Faithfully Fervent

Standing Firm as a Woman of God
in a World Ready to Run

Rhianna Marie Mitchell

CLAY BRIDGES
PRESS

Faithfully Fervent
Standing Firm as a Woman of God in a World Ready to Run

Published by Clay Bridges in Houston, TX
www.ClayBridgesPress.com

ISBN-10: 1-939815-73-8
ISBN-13: 978-1-939815-73-6
eISBN-10: 1-939815-77-0
eISBN-13: 978-1-939815-77-4

Special Sales: Most Clay Bridges titles are available in special quantity discounts. Custom imprinting or excerpting can also be done to fit special needs. Contact Clay Bridges at Info@ClayBridgesPress.com

Table of Contents

Chapter 1

Abandon

I'm taken back to a place where the floors of my own life were ripped out from under me. My body was falling as if gravity in the moment ceased to exist. Tears streaming. The most agonizing weeping, you couldn't even fathom. I could feel the pounding of my heart in my chest fighting to maintain beat after beat as I was convinced my heart had stopped. **All because of the one letter left in my hands.**

The letter left behind by my husband that told me I wasn't going to be married anymore. The letter that confirmed destroyed vows and promises. They meant *nothing* now. **The one letter that in the moment completely *destroyed me*.**

Immediately, I was taken back to the month before— **January 2018.** I had nightmares **three times** about my husband walking out on me. After the third nightmare, I remember waking up in the middle of a deep sleep, sweating and in full panic. It felt so real to me. After each nightmare, I anxiously brought it up to him with deep concern; I rarely remembered nightmares or dreams. Weekly, I was checking in with my husband to make sure everything between us was okay because of how terrifying and vivid the nightmares were. Each time I so distinctly remember him telling me, "**It's probably just Satan messing with your head.**" Something in my spirit

1

just never felt right, despite the reassurance. The scary thing is it wasn't Satan after all. I came to realize the nightmares were actually warnings from the Lord about what would lie ahead, in not even a month.

I was desperately trying to comprehend this devastation before me. I frantically replayed the events of the day before in my head to try to determine if I blatantly missed something. The night before, we had spontaneously gone on a date, driving more than 20 miles just to get donuts all the way in Frisco; I reminisced now about the laughter and the I-love-yous.

Fast-forward to the next evening; we were saying our goodbyes before work. Something was *different* about this goodbye. As my husband was about to leave, he turned around, kissed me, and randomly said, "I'm sorry." I was so confused about that "I'm sorry" but brushed it off. Following this was the phone call as we drove to work where we said our usual "See you in the morning." What I didn't realize then was that the "I'm sorry" was an encrypted "**I'm abandoning you.**"

Oh, the gash I felt, driving the dagger deeper into my stomach when I replayed those events in my head.

It didn't make any sense.

Now, looking around my half-empty apartment, I saw the broken reality that what once was didn't exist any longer. "What once was" meant two people who had come together as one, opening the door to building a life and calling this place home. These whitewashed walls carefully held memories of love and laughter in pictures that brought out color and life. These very floors had supported the weight of the marriage and the footsteps traveled. *For better or worse.*

Instead, these walls were now shattered. The floors had crumbled. Everything was gone as I was desperately hanging on by a thread. I was up for 48 hours—mind racing, heart aching. Vividly, I remember walking into the bathroom clenching in my hand some leftover muscle relaxers from a previous injury, almost believing Satan's lie that if I just took them all, my pain would be gone. If my own husband didn't want or need me, then definitely the rest of the world clearly couldn't want or need me, either.

Something stopped me.

In that moment, I fell to my knees, weeping on the floor, desperately pleading for God to rescue me. Through my agonizing, ear-splitting sobbing, I faintly muttered, "God, how can I possibly survive this? *I can't do this.*"

This was rock bottom.

Rock Bottom, the Brunt of Brokenness

When you hear the phrase *hit rock bottom*, it's fair to assume the context has a negative connotation.

Darkness. The lowest point. Excruciatingly painful. The end.

When dealing with family, friends, or relationships in which a loved one has strayed and become a prodigal, it's incredibly common to hear this: "They'll have to hit rock bottom at some point."

But why?

It's a hopeful cry of desperation that they'll come back around—come back around as the old self they once were or a completely new self exceedingly better than before. **Maybe at one point you were, or currently are, that prodigal.**

Is it not in our moments of desperation when we literally have no deeper to fall that we finally look up and cry out to Jesus that we need Him now more than ever? When you're in a moment, or season, of hitting rock bottom, it's so easy to feel defeated and believe the **lies** that Satan longs to feed you.

There's no hope.

No reason to carry on.

You've finally messed up too much this time.

There's no way you can possibly redeem yourself.

You're unforgivable.

You're not worthy.

You're completely alone.

What I find so fascinating about the term *rock bottom* is specifically the word *rock*.

Think about it. Who is our ultimate rock? *Jesus.*

It's not surprising, then, when we hear testimonies of people who finally come to the end of themselves at rock bottom. In turn, they became completely transformed by Jesus.

You have to believe, understand, and receive this truth: **There is nothing you can do to destroy God's plan for you.** Jesus wants nothing more than to open His arms up to you and welcome you home with merciful, unending love and grace.

"And while he was still a long way off, his father saw him coming. Filled with love and compassion, he ran to his son, embraced him, and kissed him. His son said to him, 'Father, I have sinned against both heaven and you, and I am no longer worthy of being called your son.' But his father said to his servants, 'Quick! Bring the finest robe in the house and put it on him. Get a ring for his finger and sandals for his feet. And kill the calf we have been fattening. We must celebrate with a feast, for this son of mine was dead and has now returned to life. He was lost, but now he is found.'"

—Luke 15:20–24

Jesus eagerly anticipates the day you choose to look up in hope and truth instead of remain facedown in the lie that your life is nothing but destitute.

My abandonment disguised itself as my life falling apart. The truth is nothing actually broke or physically crumbled beneath me.

Why? How Could This Be?

My floor didn't crumble because the foundation beneath it was Christ. The walls never shattered or wavered in the storm because they stood on the word of God. Remember that heart I told you about? That same heart that undeniably was convinced it didn't have a single beat left? It was refined. It was carefully hand-molded by Jesus Himself into the most beautiful heart that beats life again. Not just *any* life. A redemptive life. A freeing life. A believing life. A life that relentlessly pursues Jesus Christ. A life that proclaims that if Jesus is all I have, I have exceedingly more.

Ask the Bible. Ask me. I'm a walking testimony to tell you that no battle is too great for a mighty God who goes before you. You have a God who loves you and desperately longs for your heart to do the same. Give Him your life. Abandon your own plans and relentlessly pursue the plans He has for you—plans that were written before you even breathed life. I can promise you that your life will never be the same.

Rock bottom is finally putting an end to wrestling with God and creating a beginning of surrendering to God. What appears to be the end is, in return, an opportunity for a brand-new beginning. Are you at rock bottom, friend? I'll say this: I find **freedom** in rock bottom. I don't know about you, but there's no other solid ground I'd rather completely fall to my knees on than that of Jesus—my rock, my fortress, my defense.

The LORD is my rock, my fortress, and my savior;
my God is my rock, in whom I find protection.
He is my shield, the power that saves me,
and my place of safety.

—Ps. 18:2

If you've fallen, you will stand again. If you're depleted, life will fill you again. If you feel lost, you're already found. Just like me, whatever your story, God will use you 100 percent for His glory. Choose to humbly submit. I promise you'll be blessed by your testament.

Upon this rock I will build my church, and all the powers of hell will not conquer it.

—Matt. 16:18

Self-Destruction

There's nothing like walking outside your house to find your neighbor's tree branch smashed on top of your car. I received a phone call from my friend Bri one day. She told me after a storm passed through that a massive branch had broken off and just so happened to choose her car to land on. I moved in with her not too long after that occurred and one day went out to walk the dogs. My eye caught the tree that once bore the weight of that tree branch. As I continued to walk, I felt a curiosity spur inside of me as to what factors contribute to branches naturally breaking off trees.

(Side note: As you continue to read my book, you'll find that I love to answer the *whys*. That's the nerdy nurse side of me.)

This is what I learned about trees on the Gardening Know How website:

Brittle tree branches break when faced with strong winds, heavy snowfall, or ice, and they sometimes break *under their own weight.*

Branches with narrow crotch angles are weaker than those with wide angles and more susceptible to breaking.

It's best to remove branches with narrow crotches while the tree is young to prevent problems later.

This means pruning them while they are young to encourage strong structure (emphasis added).[1]

When we are weak and immature in our faith, we waver and break apart in the storms.

How often does our fall result in our own self-destruction?
We allow self-destructive behaviors to creep in, and sin struggles to become all-consuming. We lack discipline and wear a prideful arrogance that calls the community to hold us accountable at arm's-length distance.

The narrow-angled branches symbolize our narrow-mindedness when we believe we don't need God and that we'll be our own God instead. We live in a false reality that we can keep it together all on our own.

What false reality have you battled or completely succumbed to?
I'll tell you *mine.*

My life was based on my performance. My grades, my involvement, and my being a good person validated my worth—who I was or who I ultimately was capable of becoming. It was a vicious, self-destructive cycle. The problem with

1. Jackie Carroll, "Dry and Brittle Trees—What Causes Tree Branch Breaking and Brittleness," Gardening Know How, https://www.gardening knowhow.com/ornamental/trees/tgen/dry-brittle-tree-branches.htm.

trying to convince yourself that your life is perfect is that at some point, the facade fades away because it never had a foundation to stand on.

1. **Hi, my name is Control Freak.** I desperately reached for any glimpse of control over my life. At one point in my life, I was faced with several abusive situations—physically and sexually—in which I had no control. It was robbed from me. No matter how hard I tried to escape, the situation was stronger than I was. So *control* was my hope of a way out and a way to numb my pain. The planning and color-coding queen was born.

   a. It was time to fill up my schedule until I could barely breathe—get rid of time when I would have to face the trauma in my life.

   b. It was an escape from the quiet moments that would force me to admit that my life was filled with shame and consumed with people-pleasing.

   I ran from my past life by repressing my pain. Part of it—the scary part—is that it was repressed subconsciously, but the rest I intentionally chose to flee from as if it had never happened to me. I busied myself with things that prevented me from processing and fought to do anything and everything to keep my focus forward. That led to my obsessing over the next big change I could make as I drove to my destination in life. Career? Moving? New relationships? Ridding of old relationships? It was never enough. I sure wrestled Jesus for that wheel.

   My desire to constantly change things, fix things, control things, build my schedule busy, and essentially try to make most of my decisions out of my own worldly wisdom was *selfish*. My battle was so tainted by control that my vision was clouded. That's the danger with repression; it will always come to light if you don't uproot it and heal the real underlying issue.

2. **Hi, my name is Shut Down in Arguments.** I thought I was someone who was fairly decent at handling conflict, but I was wrong.

   a. As conflict arose, I became defensive or would completely shut down and isolate myself. The habit of constantly having to protect myself and defend myself as a result of my past abusive experiences came clear. In moments of disagreement, I resorted to feeling attacked. The lies in my head told me that unless someone outwardly defended me, they automatically had to be against me.

   It was a lie because scripture clearly states that we don't battle against flesh and blood but against the enemy, Satan (Eph. 6:12). I learned that it was my coping mechanism, and I allowed Satan to take hold of something I was so vulnerable in. Yet it doesn't serve as an excuse. I exhausted myself trying to find the remedy, but I was the stumbling block in my own way.

3. **Hi, my name is Please Validate Me.** I was empty. What I failed to see was that I felt empty because only Jesus could heal and complete me.

   a. I was negative, fixated on my pain and wounds, and remained in complacency. Because of this emptiness, I didn't feel good enough or worthy enough to be the godly woman I had envisioned myself to become. I didn't believe I could ever live up to the person God had called me to be.

   b. I felt there was no point; I was simply worthless. That started the cycle of *depending on the love of others* to make me feel like somebody. I heavily relied on my husband's expression or acts of love to believe I was really worthy, but in the end it became idolatry. I couldn't look to my husband or other people to be my savior or even place that burden on someone. It's unrealistic, and it's absolutely unbiblical.

4. **Hi, my name is Manipulated by Materialism.**

Investing confidence in financial or materialistic things robs you of the freedom Christ died to bring. I let materialism manipulate me. Don't get me wrong, having or desiring really nice things is not always bad. But it's imperative to maintain an awareness that it is not taking root and becoming a heart issue.

No one can serve two masters. For you will hate one and love the other; you will be devoted to one and despise the other. You cannot serve God and be enslaved to money.

—Matt. 6:24

I had my own fair share of battles with financial status and security. It became an ugly idol. This idol conformed my identity to the likeness of the world and made me my own enemy.

I was driven to have my dream car (an Explorer) because it looked like a Range Rover.

   a. I was driven to go back to school to become a nurse practitioner to get better hours and a higher salary.
   b. I was driven to believe that going on fun trips would give me the opportunity to escape my problems or the things I was avoiding.
   c. I was driven not to tithe because I was so worried about building a significant financial security blanket, yet I made sure I had money for the things I deemed worthy superficially.

What a stab—worthy! Isn't it sad how easily we can find ourselves so entitled? Truth is, we deserve absolutely nothing, but our Savior gave us everything. How is it that I could be so consumed doing what was "best for me" while I completely neglected praising my Savior for how He had blessed me. He blessed me so I could bless others, not live for self.

> *"Bring all the tithes into the storehouse so there will be enough food in my Temple. If you do," says the LORD of Heaven's Armies, "I will open the windows of heaven for you. I will pour out a blessing so great you won't have enough room to take it in! Try it! Put me to the test!"*
>
> —Mal. 3:10

Enter Conviction

- I started tithing. I sold my dream car. I withdrew from nurse practitioner school. I moved to the suburbs and gave up city life.
- When my paycheck comes, my first 10 percent is now immediately tithed before any other financial obligation—no matter how scary it may seem. I can affirm without a doubt that God will provide and bless me. Scripture says so.
- He knew I didn't need the fancy car. He knew I wasn't meant to be a nurse practitioner but instead wanted me to pursue ministry. He knew I didn't need a high-rise because He wanted me to have an extra room to better serve His people who may have a need.

I gave up several material things that were significantly driving me, and today I feel freer than free. I learned it was more important to spend less time making our lives look pretty and instead make our hearts and how we steward others pretty.

My prayer is that you, too, will search your heart and ask Him to reveal if there's anything that could use a little "less of me." Trust me, God has no problem giving us a dose of humility.

God convicts us each differently but longs to do it lovingly.

Take a moment to sit and reflect on this: What names belong to you?

Maybe your names sound a lot like mine. Maybe there are some names you've been in denial about for quite some time. It's important to discover the names and pains we've been bound by so we know what to be freed from.

A good way to practice this accountability is to keep in check where your driving factor comes from:

- Does it drive you closer to Jesus, or does it dig a hole deeper into sin?
- Does it drive you to work hard to convince people you're happy when, in reality, you're nothing but empty?
- Does it drive you to be selfish in places you should be selfless?
- Does it drive dependence on the world or on the One who created the world?

It's important to keep tabs on the places you find your deepest drive in selfishness. It's in those places that God is trying to show you that there is something in you that needs to be humbled and renewed.

Wherever your treasure is, there the desires of your heart will also be.

—Matt. 6:21

Get rid of the false reality that we can keep it all together on our own. Choose to prune away those thoughts and stand firm as a child of God. Get ready to abandon those names by embarking on a transformative journey that will declare you are clean and free in Jesus's name.

Throw off your old sinful nature and your former way of life, which is corrupted by lust and deception. Instead, let the Spirit renew your thoughts and attitudes. Put on your new nature, created to be like God—truly righteous and holy.

—Eph. 4:22–24

Abandon and Obey

Jesus obeyed unto death. Would you be willing to obey if coming to the end of yourself meant committing to the death of your will, your plans, and your ways? You are probably feeling a sense of hesitation as you ask yourself this question.

Why is that?

Because our entire lives have been based on doing and planning things when we want them and how we want them. We're so quick to whip out our calendars and cultivate dreams in the midst of telling God, "Thanks, God, but I got this." He called me to be strong anyway, right? I can handle it.

The problem is just that—*we handle it.* How many times did people in the Bible decide to go their own way despite clear direction and instruction to go God's way? It's quite humorous that we actually think we know what is best for us. Surely, we can comprehend more than the God who molded us with His very hands—the same God who created the entire universe on His own.

In the beginning of my journey, I felt led to challenge myself to read the entire Bible in 90 days, front cover to back cover. Coming across Abraham in the Old Testament, I was incredibly drawn to him. I was in awe because this man faced constant adversity but kept hearing God say go, and he went. Here's the thing. Abraham also wrestled with doing things his way. He, too, was human, but something changed when he decided to ultimately choose God's way.

I'd done enough doing things my way; instead, I desperately wanted to live by faith. Unwavering faith. I wanted a faith like Abraham's.

The promises God gave to Abraham, to humans, appeared completely impossible and illogical. The greatest promise was that God declared that Abraham would be the father of the nations. Abraham had long periods of waiting. He clung for dear life to God's promise to keep pushing through.

Let us hold tightly without wavering to the hope we affirm, for God can be trusted to keep his promise.

—Heb. 10:23

That's why Abraham's faith empowered me so much. He had **every reason** to quit, and his battles were surely much more debilitating and trying than mine could ever be. If he could do it, then why shouldn't I?

Look at what Abraham endured, just to list a few:

He is called out of his comfort zone by going to Canaan.

He is faced with a massive famine.

His wife gets surrendered to Pharaoh.

He is separated from his son Ishmael.

God asks him to sacrifice his son Isaac.

Despite facing these trials, look at what scripture tells us about his response:

Even when there was no reason for hope, Abraham kept hoping—believing that he would become the father of many nations. For God had said to him, "That's how many descendants you will have!" And Abraham's faith did not weaken....Abraham never wavered in believing God's promise. In fact, his faith grew stronger, and in this he brought glory to God.

—Rom. 4:18–20

Like Abraham, we need to have a drive for that radical faith and obedience. It may look completely illogical right now. It may even look impossible. But what we must not forget is that God defies all logic and thrives on making the impossible possible. He loves to bless you with breakthroughs. Don't let your current circumstances pressure you to give up.

Patiently endure and trust that God is determined to fulfill His promises.

I've come to find in my own experiences of choosing my will and way that I've ultimately been rooted in fear. If I can somewhat control the process, then just maybe I won't face rejection, suffering, loss, failure, or heartbreak. You can make all the plans and decisions and even plot out your ability to control the situation, but you may still be faced with the completely opposite outcome.

When we abandon our plans, submit to becoming obedient, and faithfully trust in God's promises, we will never be put to shame. He will use each and every trial to bring greater glory to His name. So, friends, let us abandon and obey.

We can rejoice, too, when we run into problems and trials, for we know that they help us develop endurance. And endurance develops strength of character, and character strengthens our confident hope of salvation. And this hope will not lead to disappointment. For we know how dearly God loves us, because he has given us the Holy Spirit to fill our hearts with his love.

—Rom. 5:3–5

Raw and Real

Being a Christian isn't about pretty, put-together prayers. Sometimes, if not most times, our prayers should be filled with honest, gut-wrenching tears.

It's raw. It's *real*.

We live under this false pretense that it gets easier when we decide to become a believer. It's easy to pull out scripture and pour out truth when you're not the one desperately grasping for an ounce of a breakthrough. It's easy to say "trust God" when you're not the one hanging by the thread of only having "just God." It's easy to say, "I'm doing okay" to fight off the pride in humbly saying, "I honestly don't know how to make it through another day."

But among the brutal, honest, tears, I can say firsthand that you end up being met by the God who knows exactly how to calm your fears. The God who hears you. The God who sees you. The God who believes in you.

> *Give your burdens to the LORD,*
> *and he will take care of you.*
> *He will not permit the godly to slip and fall.*
>
> —Ps. 55:22

Maybe right now you're not okay. Maybe right now you need to hear it's okay if you're really not okay. Maybe you've picked up this book because you need even the faintest glimpse of hope. What I can tell you is that there is a reason our paths have crossed. There is a reason you were led to this book. On these pages, I will fiercely fight to tell you that God with his goodness, mercy, and faithful heart never intends for you to stay in that place of not being okay. There will be a day that your tears of mourning will radically become transformed into tears of rejoicing and adoring. Some days and nights you may find yourself clenching your Bible and earnestly seeking a place to rest your head.

My beautiful friend, it's completely okay, because it's in the midst of the raw, real, dependence that you can experience the fulfillment of His promises. That was true for me many days and nights. In full transparency, it still can be me. Your growth in the Lord shouldn't make you more confident in self, but it should drive the roots of your dependence on God deeper. I'm okay being in this place every once in a while, but Lord, how I *praise You* and *thank You* for setting this captive 100 percent free. My prayer for you, too, my friend, is that you will rejoice in the gift of freedom—freely gifted to you—to heal you.

The choice is yours. Are you willing to surrender all hope out of fear because of the adversity that lies before you? No! I declare you a warrior and that you're ready to learn what it takes to instead faithfully and fervently stand firm, find freedom, and **fight**.

You're about to take what the enemy *intended* to use to try to destroy you, to declare that God is going to transform you and your circumstances into good.

You intended to harm me, but God intended it all for good. He brought me to this position so I could save the lives of many people.

—Gen. 50:20

Chapter 2

Humbled

What does it mean to become humble? According to Dictionary.com, *humble* is "having a feeling of insignificance, inferiority, subservience."

Would you use the word *humble* to define yourself? Or is it a word needed to refine you? It is not in our innate nature to deny self as much as we so quickly are prone to choose self. Our own importance, rather, is held to the utmost highest estimate. We enter into situations immediately trying to decipher how it could benefit us or harm us. If it doesn't have any effect on us, then it will easily have no part of us.

Me. Me. Me.

When you think of selfishness, you're probably more likely to point out a character flaw in someone else rather than in yourself. Someone you know may have even come to mind just now. For myself, I never questioned the possibility of being selfish, because in my head, I saw myself as genuinely servant-hearted. Servant-hearted people, of course, can't be selfish, right? Wrong. Do you know that the root of all sin actually lies in selfishness? Therefore, if you sin, which all of us do, you're selfish. We're selfish because we're fallen.

When we were controlled by our old nature, sinful desires were at work within us, and the law aroused these evil desires that produced a harvest of sinful deeds, resulting in death. But now we have been released from the law, for we died to it and are no longer captive to its power. Now we can serve God, not in the old way of obeying the letter of the law, but in the new way of living in the Spirit. And I know that nothing good lives in me, that is, in my sinful nature. I want to do what is right, but I can't. I want to do what is good, but I don't. I don't want to do what is wrong, but I do it anyway. But if I do what I don't want to do, I am not really the one doing wrong; it is sin living in me that does it.

—Rom. 7:5–6, 18–20

I desired to gain insight into the depth of our fallen nature and how we are instead called to conquer our sin by allowing Christ to powerfully move through us to stop *desiring* sin. Sin, while enticing, is ultimately fleeting.

And what was the result? You are now ashamed of the things you used to do, things that end in eternal doom.

—Rom. 6:21

Scripture warns us of the importance of praying through our reactions and decisions. A solid accountability check is to ask yourself, **Will this honor God?** Or am I going to harm myself in the process by fueling selfishness and self-gratification leading only to shame and regret?

For Christ also suffered once for sins, the righteous for the unrighteous, to bring you to God. He was put to death in the body but made alive in the Spirit.

—1 Pet. 3:18 NIV

Christ ultimately conquered our sin by His sacrifice on the cross. Because of His sacrifice, we are no longer bound to death by sin. But we are still held accountable to cut ties with our sinful vices. That consists of stripping our pride by acknowledging our faults, coming forth in sincere repentance to the Lord, and trusting Him to transform our hearts and minds to become more like Him.

People who conceal their sins will not prosper,
   but if they confess and turn from them, they will receive mercy.
Blessed are those who fear to do wrong,
   but the stubborn are headed for serious trouble.
                                                    —Prov. 28:13–14

You truly will not be able to fight to overcome your sin unless you feel the weight of the burden it carries. Once the pain and awareness of the destruction your sin carries is inflicted heavily upon you, then you stop desiring to cross that sinful path again. It's not about trying harder or attempting to gain God's approval, because Jesus died to cancel that out. Instead, you are called to seek the Lord and ask Him to help you fight against your sin.

Unfortunately, this is not a quick-fix method. It's one you learn to acquire and carry with you through your life. Just because we grow in our relationship with the Lord does not exempt us from battling the temptation of previous sin struggles. In fact, the temptations may tend to get stronger as the enemy tries to take you down, but you learn to fight that much harder to obtain the ultimate victory through Christ alone.

If you choose to live in denial, you will never take hold of the root. Without knowledge of the root in sin struggles, sin continues to rebirth itself. When we know the root, we know exactly how to fight. We must stand firm, take hold of the root, and completely uproot the sin if we want to live a life of humility and one that honors Christ.

After acquiring this insight, I devoted several weeks to taking on the incredibly difficult task of pleading with God to humble me. I desperately longed to understand where and how I had been falling short as a woman of God. "Lord, where is this rooted?" I asked. I prayed for the Lord to give me His eyes to see, His ears to hear, and His wisdom for understanding. This, my friends, was far more challenging than many other tasks I've faced in my life. But God showed up in a mighty way. If you ask Him for wisdom and understanding, He promises to give it to you.

> *"Keep on asking, and you will receive what you ask for. Keep on seeking, and you will find. Keep on knocking, and the door will be opened to you. For everyone who asks, receives. Everyone who seeks, finds. And to everyone who knocks, the door will be opened."*
>
> —Matt. 7:7–8

He met me in my pain and revealed things completely unimaginable. While it was incredibly painful, it was at the same time the most healing and freeing experience I could have asked for. The Lord in His goodness and mercy took the utmost traumatic time of my life and used it for His glory by making it into the most powerfully transformative time of my life. If I had not allowed the mighty role the humbling had played, I'm not sure I would have fully and freely surrendered before Him. Once you can admit your faults, flaws, and sin struggles, you're ready to take the next step in the battle by going through refinement.

Create in me a clean heart, O God.
Renew a loyal spirit within me.

—Ps. 51:10

Refinement

If you think about the process of refinement, it's reasonable to believe that it would be a meticulous and painful process. Wendy, my counselor, shared with me a story about the beauty found in refinement. She told me to envision a china teapot, one that sparkled and one you couldn't resist picking up with the aspiration of taking it home. Imagine, then, if the teapot could tell you its story—the story of how it became glistening and beautiful. Before the handcrafted colors and shine were carefully designed, there stood a pile of dark, rugged clay. The clay had to be shaped at just the right consistency, or it would become too stiff and unmoldable, or too wet and destructible.

An artist cautiously shapes and smoothes the clay by kneading it to create the shape and design envisioned. Once the shape is just right, it is placed into a kiln at a scorching high temperature. For the clay to be classified as pottery, it must endure this particular fire that produces permanent change. All the properties the clay once had are significantly altered as a result of the heat. The once-rugged pile of clay now has a purpose as a teapot. Once the purpose has been established, the creator designs patterns and chooses colors. Creation is then complete.

When you see people filled with joy and colorful lives, you can't help but become drawn to them. It's hard not to admire their beauty. How much more beautiful do they become when you learn the story that brought them to choose that joy?

You suddenly develop a deeper appreciation for them. They may have gone through a painful fire, but that fire solidified a **magnified strength. A magnified beauty. A magnified dependence on their Creator.** They trusted that their Creator would know exactly when their time in the fire was complete and when they should be rescued from the heat. They may have had all their properties altered in the fire, but they came out looking like the One who called them higher.

And some of the wise will fall victim to persecution. In this way, they will be refined and cleansed and made pure until the time of the end, for the appointed time is still to come.

—Dan. 11:35

In refinement, we're called to take the properties of our sin and lay them at the foot of the cross. We are, instead, acknowledging our selfishness and asking for forgiveness, humbly basking in the awareness that our sin isn't counted against us because of the One who died selflessly. Humbling ourselves burns. But with each degree endured, scorched away are those characteristics that defy Christ—characteristics that kept us dark, rugged, and in the bondage of inconsistency. We become molded, firm, and embellished by grace, joy, freedom, and humility.

Being pummeled to ashes may be initially seen as defeat, and some may see it as tragedy. I see it as a trajectory. Because of our resurrected King, He graciously singes the darkness off you and out of you and places it in a pile before you. When you stare at the pile, fear may incline you to reach back and grasp what God is telling you to let go of. You can scoop up and grasp all you want, but the ashes eventually slip right

back through your hands. These ashes were never yours to
hold. As the ashes finish slipping through your fingers, keep
your palms open wide and watch what God is about to do
before your eyes.

*Then the Lord God formed the man from the dust of the ground.
He breathed the breath of life into the man's nostrils, and the
man became a living person.*

—Gen. 2:7

Did you catch the part that says it's in the state of dust that
he breathes in life? If our entire being had a beginning from
nothing but dust, do our ashes not continue to give us hope
that God will use this to form yet an entirely new beginning?

We have the choice. Are we going to allow refinement
to keep us wallowing and suffocating in our ashes? Or will
we choose to dust off the ashes, turn them into beauty, and
graciously choose instead to grow? He creates beauty out of
even the darkest ashes.

*To all who mourn in Israel,
    he will give a crown of beauty for ashes,
a joyous blessing instead of mourning,
    festive praise instead of despair.
In their righteousness, they will be like great oaks
    that the Lord has planted for his own glory.*

—Isa. 61:3

Growth

When you think about poison ivy, you probably associate it
with something toxic. You envision it looking like a shrub,
probably very low to the ground. Did you know that poison
ivy actually has the potential to grow into a vine? For it to

become a vine, it has to develop support and solid roots. Like vines, we have the choice to determine the direction of our growth. Because it is in a vine's nature to grow in different directions, pruning is an incredibly imperative part of the growth process.

Pruning encourages vines to remain healthy, enhances productivity, and most importantly keeps them from spiraling out of control. If pruning is not utilized early on in the growth process, vines become at risk for completely collapsing beneath themselves.[1] When we are succumbing to the toxic things in our life, we are hindered in growth. We stay low to the ground instead of rising upward.

Reflect on the toxic things that may be in your life right now.
What things aren't honoring to God?
What things aren't ultimately rooted in the Lord?
Toxic things can consist of your sin, relationships, job, hobbies, habits, or even material items, to list just a few.

Be encouraged that although we each have toxic vices that need pruning, if our roots go deep into the Lord, we still have a chance of rising.

Let your roots grow down into him, and let your lives be built on him. Then your faith will grow strong in the truth you were taught, and you will overflow with thankfulness.

—Col. 2:7

Will we stay complacent and blend in? Or will we choose to prune away sin and grow upward to become more like

1. Karen Davis Cutler, "How to Prune Your Vines and Other Climbing Plants," September 8, 2003, Brooklyn Botanic Garden, https://www.bbg.org/gardening/article/pruning_plants_that_ascend.

Him? God will fight for you and keep you together. Don't fool yourself into thinking you can do it alone. He will be your structure and your strength.

"Yes, I am the vine; you are the branches. Those who remain in me, and I in them, will produce much fruit. For apart from me you can do nothing."

—John 15:5

Rejection

Aside from handling our own sin, there is not much that is in our control. Rejection just so happens to be one of those things. If you want a direct flight to destination humbled, simply hop on the rejection express. Rejection is one of the most painful experiences that has the ability to completely bring us down to our knees. In complete transparency, I can share with you what rejection did to me and the lies that completely tormented me.

I wasn't good enough. I wasn't godly enough. I wasn't beautiful enough.

I wasn't worth the commitment.

I didn't deserve for better or for worse.

I wasn't worthy to be fought for.

I wasn't worthy to be respected or cherished.

I deserved this abandonment, this rejection.

This was all because of me.

Surely, no one could love me.

Rejection fuels the lies that drive spirit-deep into us. We tend to live in our own little world where we couldn't possibly be wrong, and we allow our egos to manifest so strongly. Oh, and don't forget about denial. I told myself that this surely could never happen to me. It doesn't happen to people like me. I wouldn't marry just to become a divorcée.

Rejection has a way of opening our eyes to see that maybe we aren't as perfect as we've perceived ourselves after all. As I battled those lies, I became overwhelmed by humility when I recognized the magnitude of what Christ really did for me. How is it that I can sit in my distress of rejection while thinking I'm so self-righteous that I couldn't deserve this? There is no greater rejection a person can face on this planet than what Christ faced. Hanging on the cross, beaten, spit on, verbally persecuted—for whom? For what? Sinners. *You and me.*

So then, what's the truth?

Someone could love me. Jesus loved me for me.

He chose rejection and abandonment for me.

He chose this because I was worthy enough in his eyes to be fought for and worthy to be cherished infinitely.

He fought for me because He knew I deserved more.

For better or worse, He committed to me by hanging on the cross at Calvary.

Despite Christ's ultimate rejection, it never once steered Him off mission. If this was Christ's calling, then so it must be for you and me. A lot of the time, our encounters with rejection taint our beliefs on how God sees us. If imperfect people can reject us, how can we truly be accepted by an infinitely perfect God?

I had an encounter with a homeless man that perfectly depicted how we allow our fear of unworthiness and rejection to hinder gracious acceptance. He approached me on the evening of **October 21, 2018**, when I was in downtown Fort Worth. I had offered him a ride to his shelter because he would have been walking the entire night to get there.

As I approached my car, I realized it was a complete mess because the back seat was covered everywhere with hair from both of my dogs. I immediately tried to clean off the seat as best I could. I know how much I hate my dog hair, and I surely didn't want him to have to deal with it as well. While I was scraping the seat, he looked at me with the sincerest yet defeated eyes and said, "You don't have to do that; I'm already dirty." My heart sank. I told him, "You deserve to sit in a clean seat, and I won't settle for anything less."

Isn't that the exact thing Jesus says to us? We tell Jesus, "I'm already dirty, and I don't deserve to be clean." It doesn't matter how rejected, outcast, or dirty you've been, all He's pleading with you to do is come and let His redemption begin.

I was fully convinced I could never get past the brutal dagger that rejection drove into me. How could I? Where would I even begin? Often we allow shame to swallow us whole and isolate us in a place we can't even bring ourselves to speak of. Our pride forces rejection into repression in the attempt to move forward and pretend it never happened. Reality is that we don't overcome rejection by avoiding it. We overcome it by completely surrendering it to the One who ultimately conquered it. No one has the power to define or determine our worth or value because Christ died for us. He fervently ordained our worth.

Don't allow pain of rejection, fear, or pride to stop you from pursuing your mission to glorify Christ. View rejection as an opportunity for God's mighty power to be magnified. While the enemy tries to use rejection to destroy you, your mighty God stands before you to restore you. To stand firm, you have to see past the lies, humble yourself against self-righteousness and pride, and view yourself through Christ's eyes.

*Jesus was "rejected indeed by men, but chosen by God."
(1 Pet. 2:4 WEB) The rejection of man is meaningless if God's
favor is upon you.*

—Bob Sorge

Judgment Seat

October 10, 2018, was the day I sold my ring, and in return,
I was gifted with a very profound experience. As I sat down
and pulled out my ring box to hand it to the man at the diamond company, the weight of the small black box suddenly
became increasingly heavier. I felt myself handing over the
last physical remnant of my marriage. He opened the box
and carefully placed the ring between the grasp of his fingers,
examining the size, the shape, and the band. It was as if his
gaze bore so deeply into this ring that he could visualize the
marriage that once was bound by it on my fourth left finger.
That finger was supposed to continue wearing that ring to
symbolize a promised covenant and commitment.

Moments passed, and he slowly took out his magnifying
glass. He told me he had to examine the diamond carefully
to determine its clarity. As I blankly stared at his meticulous
examination, he looked up at me with caution and hesitation.
It was time for the final step in deeming the overall worth.
To do so, the diamond had to be removed from the band to
determine the weight it carried alone. The moment he pried
the diamond out of the setting, my heart completely dropped.
It was like witnessing the visual representation of my marriage
being torn apart. The diamond was originally placed into a
setting for support and protection. Little did I know that years
later it would lead to the most heartbreaking rejection.

I pondered my thoughts as I walked out of the store
and spent some time with the Lord. When I reflected on the

process of my ring examination, I recognized how similar it was to the day when we will face our own judgment before the throne of God. How humbling it was to recognize that the account I will one day give is solely based on me alone, just as the diamond's worth was determined on its own.

I realized that it didn't matter how anyone treated me but how I responded. How I chose to be like Jesus despite the pain that was inflicted. How I served and how I loved. Was my behavior biblical or resentful? It was in those moments that I had to humble myself and recognize that the only person I can control is me. There was no more room for justification or selfish excuses. It no longer was about being right. Instead, it became about becoming more like Christ. My decisions, actions, and behaviors would all have to be answered for someday. On that someday, I wanted to be able to hear His words, "Well done, good and faithful servant, for standing on My word."

God sees each and every one of us extravagantly more beautiful than we will ever see a diamond. But under the bright shining light and magnifying glass, ask yourself this: What in your life will be reflected?

Does the light that shines into you glisten just as brightly outside of you?

Is there a profound clarity that you lived out the gospel in full transparency?

Or was it just focused inwardly and selfishly?

How you choose to faithfully live for God's kingdom is where the weight of your true value lies.

You must all be quick to listen, slow to speak, and slow to get angry. Human anger does not produce the righteousness God desires. So get rid of all the filth and evil in your lives, and

*humbly accept the word God has planted in your hearts, for it
has the power to save your souls. But don't just listen to God's
word. You must do what it says. Otherwise, you are only fooling
yourselves.*

—James 1:19–22

Gratitude in the Grumbling

One of the last greatest challenges I learned in humbling was
how to stop grumbling. There was so much beauty in turning to gratitude in the moments I least wanted to. Wendy
encouraged me to express gratitude daily. I initially didn't
think that could make a big impact among the other things
I had challenged myself to do. But when I started to do this,
I was immaculately surprised.

I started to see life differently. The good and bad are all
just temporary. When you shift your thoughts and recognize
the truth that each and every spiritual gift, job, relationship,
and possession comes from the Lord, you start to cherish them
much more. Joy seemed to flow more freely. I could appreciate
each and every ounce of beauty around me. I could choose
to praise the Lord for the promises I knew were yet to come,
despite the storm that was trying to keep me worn down.

Worship is a powerful weapon to combat grumbling.
Have you ever noticed that when you're really struggling,
worship music becomes even more calming and empowering? There were days when I could barely fight emotionally
to see the silver lining. Weeping, completely on my knees. It
was in those moments on my knees that I turned on some
worship music and realized I was in the best position I could
ever be. One of the most powerful songs I clung to in those
moments was "Though You Slay Me" by Shane & Shane.

I highly encourage you to listen to it. If you're able to, sit and meditate on the power of the words to that song, and then reflect on how you will personally choose to see God in difficult times or during your current season of pain.

Our hardships and trials don't negate who God is. God is always good amid our suffering. When we choose to praise Him despite our suffering, we are boldly declaring that we believe the Lord's promises are true.

Pray this with me:
This may be the most gut-wrenching pain, but, God, I believe You will bring healing.
This may be the most fearful time, but, God, I believe You will powerfully rescue me.
This may be the greatest time of uncertainty, but, God, I believe in the path You've paved for me.

> *We must accept finite disappointment, but never lose infinite hope.*
>
> —Martin Luther King Jr.

We seem to not have difficulty asking God for the things we aspire to have or aspire to become. How often, though, do we really sit still and fathom the beauty in what He has already done? Each and every person is blessed differently. It's easy to think that if I just had what others had, maybe I would be happy. In return, also recognize that people are saying the same thing about you.

Take some time to reflect on your blessings.
What could you be more grateful for?
What have you been blessed with that you may have over-looked completely?

What relationships have you taken for granted?

What areas of your life could use less grumbling and more praising?

By focusing on giving thanks and praise, you are continuously pursuing to live out the gracious and tender heart you initially asked God to give you. Sometimes we think that being strong alone is what we're called to do; but in humbleness and tenderness, our weakness becomes a strength that allows our hearts to fall into complete submission with the Lord.

We finally start believing "your will, not mine" is genuinely what's best. We believe a closed door is because there is something worth so much more. In moments when we're stressed or feel completely alone, we're reminded that we're blessed and that we always have the mighty King seated on the throne. When we stand firm by choosing to walk humbly and appreciate genuinely, we're ready then to love much more selflessly.

> *Give thanks to the LORD, for he is good!*
> *His faithful love endures forever.*
>
> —Ps. 107:1

Chapter 3

Becoming Love

What have you done to deserve the most impeccable love of Christ? Nothing. Absolutely nothing. What, then, could you do to lose it?

Christ's love never fades, never wavers, sees the good, perseveres, and challenges you to be and do better. It is a love that looks past faults and failures and sees you as nothing short of the prize of His eyes. You could do absolutely nothing for Him, yet He chose to infinitely do more than fathomable for you.

Would you choose love if you were fully aware that your love would not be reciprocated? Would you choose love if it meant slowly and painfully stripping off pride layer by layer? Would you choose love to serve someone else and sanctify yourself in the process?

This recurring theme is quite powerful, and it's a choice. One of the most profound realizations about scripture is that it never encourages you to base commands on emotion; rather, you're called to act, obey, and choose to become love, no matter how difficult or exhausting the circumstances may be.

Why is love so powerful and yet can be so painful? Because of what Jesus did. Dying on a cross was a sacrifice.

It was painful. It was debilitating. It was the ultimate depiction of love.

Jesus chose to face adversity, while we so easily turn away from it. He selflessly says, "Because I love you," while we say, "But I love me." He saw joy in "love thy neighbor," yet we frequently groan and plead, "What about me?"

Press into the Lord and ask, "How can I humble myself and love someone better?"
Maybe it's a relationship you've contemplated reconciling. Maybe it looks like loving someone you once deemed unlovable. Challenge yourself by being Jesus to someone, and start with a newfound love.

> *Live a life filled with love, following the example of Christ. He loved us and offered himself as a sacrifice for us, a pleasing aroma to God.*
>
> —Eph. 5:2

Why Do It?
So, then, *how* do we love?

Because I mentioned that love is a choice, I want to bring into full awareness and transparency that it is not an easy one. If it were easy, we could love incredibly freely and without inconvenience. Love doesn't come immediately, either. It takes a lot of patience, time, and work.

While that may sound exhausting, especially if you feel you're beyond your limit in what more you could possibly give, I will preface and promise you that it is the most healing and freeing thing you can do. This is coming from firsthand experience. Instead of listening to the world's enticement and invitation to completely give up on my marriage, I faithfully followed the Lord's call for me to stand firm and fight for it. It was a 229-day arduous journey—one that I had to choose to commit to *daily*. I never *had* to do what I did as I stood for unconditional love. Because I fully submitted my heart to the Lord, I was met with heavy convictions about the decisions I made. Would I choose to become more like Jesus or more like the world?

If you make the choice to fight for love, not only are you going to bring glory to Jesus, but you may be doing it for many reasons you may have never realized. First, you do it simply for yourself so you have the ability to grow and find freedom. You do it for the people watching you. For the people you don't even realize you will become a witness and testament to. For the people who claim to know Jesus, but their life has never shown genuine conviction until they heard about you—what you've done and what you could do. **And ultimately for the people who may not even know Jesus, until you.**

That's why you do it.

On **June 25, 2018**, I will never forget what Zach, Bri's husband, said that night to our married community group. He said, "I think we all can attest that we have grown to love Rhianna's husband more and more each day just by witnessing the way she has shown her sacrificial love for him."

If you want to become and look more like Christ, you have to ask yourself if you are willing to make mighty sacrifices. To answer this, you more than likely will ask, "What exactly am I sacrificing in the process?

Time. Selfishness. Bitterness. Resentment. Victimization. Self-loathing. Discontentment. Chains. Burdens. Suffering. Rejection. Retaliation.

Those are all pretty heavy things. You may not understand, or you may be confused about why some of the things you sacrifice appear incredibly negative. Wouldn't you want to get rid of those things? Absolutely! No-brainer. But I challenge you to look in the mirror.

How often are we so quick to say this instead:

"If it doesn't benefit me, then it won't have anything to do with me."

"They don't deserve me; I deserve better."

"I'm just wasting my time if it doesn't end the way I want or need it to."

"I want them to feel the same pain they caused me."

"They don't deserve happiness when they made my life look like this."

"I'm not going out of my way. If they want me, they'll come to me."

"Why me? Why does this always happen to just me?"

"What did I do to deserve this?"

"I'll show them life was much better without them anyway."

"Then they'll be sorry for the hurt they caused me."

I know these statements all too well because this used to be me. The selfishness that brewed inside of me was intoxicating. I was that person who said I want to walk with Jesus but found inconvenience and sacrifice too much for me. If someone hurt me, then goodbye; you don't deserve me.

But let me tell you this. When I finally chose to lay down my selfishness and control before the throne, God took all I had left to give and transformed it into a mighty gift. I welled up with a flood-worthy amount of tears, fought against my convictions at times, but then cried out to Jesus, "Please, help me do this." And He did.

We can be very quick to underestimate the power, healing, and freedom Jesus can give. Most of the blessings I had in front of me were blocked by my own inability to ask Jesus, "Can you do this for me?"

The only thing that kept me going during this time was clinging to the promises that Jesus would bless my call and obedience to love with Christ-like love.

Cease the Compromise

On **August 29, 2018**, I was having one of those days when the heartache just wouldn't release no matter what I did. Later that day, I sat alone with the Lord, desperately pleading for a breath of relief from this agony. When I walked into my closet, I was immediately drawn to the box where I kept memorable items. For some reason, I felt this inclination to read the letters my husband and I had written to each other when we first started dating. We felt led to write these letters as our basis for communication because we wanted to keep our primary focus on the Lord and not on each other. In my head, I felt like maybe I needed to see these letters to convince myself that I must have somehow overlooked some massive red flag or foreshadowing that my marriage was a mistake.

But you know how God works. He usually shows you the complete opposite of what you think you will discover. I'm going to share with you a couple of excerpts from the very first letter I wrote to my husband.

August 12, 2015

My complacency clouded me from believing Jesus could and would seek me for a challenge. From that moment, you were a challenge to my faith and relationship with Christ...*you* *encourage me to fight for myself and all that I stand for...***no one has ever challenged me the way you do** (emphasis added).

Here's where it gets scary:

I **promise to pray** for you *every single day*. I promise to continue to live my life with grace and dignity. For if that day comes and you are my husband, I *want to honor you* and make you proud....I can promise you to always **fight for what is just**. I can promise you **I would love you like Jesus**, challenge you, and pursue your heart and spirit daily....We will always **seek Him first**. I can promise you **I will fight to do so** (emphasis added).

The Lord used this moment to really convict my heart. He convicted me because He reminded me that this is the woman of God He created in me. He knew I could draw strength from this. I was faced with yet another powerful choice to make. Would I back down not only on my vows but also on my promises from day one, just because my husband did? I had to remember in my heart that I had made these vows and statements because I genuinely meant them with all I had. Now, more than ever, I was faced with a true test of my character, promises, and integrity. Who knew that three years after writing the letter, I would be faithfully fighting to fulfill each and every promise?

What you need to remember is that it's never too late to take a stand to uphold who you're called to be. I made the choice to stand on my word. My friend, even though it may be difficult right now, you have the power through Christ to do the same. Just because someone fails you, hurts you, betrays you, gives up on you, or abandons you, you don't have to compromise all that God instilled and created in you.

My husband should have fought for me the way I fervently fought for him, but he didn't. Maybe right now you're in a place of deep hurt because your person or your people aren't fighting, won't fight, or didn't fight for you, too. Don't allow them or the situation to blame you, shame you, destroy you, or define you. The world will tell us to compromise all that Christ would call us to do by just saying "move on" or "treat them just as badly." But we aren't of the world; we've been called higher. We're going completely countercultural with this one.

You're a fighter, and you won't let that person or people stop you from the mission to which God has called you. I had to keep reminding myself that my fight in the end wasn't about or entirely for just my husband, but ultimately for Christ.

Take a step back from your situation or circumstance and ask the Lord in prayer to give you His eyes to see. There is something God wants to show you and bring out of you in this season of learning for you to become love.

I want to empower you by challenging you to become love to those who have significantly hurt you. Because I've been there, I'm fully aware of how difficult that is and that it is so important to continue to give yourself grace. You are learning to rewire your brain in thought processes and in actions. It's not our natural response because we have conditioned ourselves to live in sin from birth due to the fall of humankind. There will be times when you want to give up. You may face utter exhaustion because you aren't seeing immediate results, or you might be struggling to see how or where this is benefiting you. If I could only tell you the number of times I cried out to God, "What's the point?" But I felt like I was constantly giving of myself, hurting myself even more than just letting go.

That's a worldly perspective I had. What I didn't realize was that the Lord was working out a radical transformation in my heart throughout the entire process. A shift began in me that spurred me on to desire to love hard and love well. The selfishness in my heart began to slowly die off. When I chose to love and pray for my enemy, I started to feel free. I began to shift my thoughts and heart from "It's what I'm supposed to do" to "It's what I *want* to do." I'm so passionate about this because I know and have seen the impeccable blessing and freedom readily awaiting me on the other side.

Christ continues to fight for us despite the number of times we have said or may say again, "I don't need you" or "I don't want anything to do with you." If He doesn't give up on that selfish version that can live within me, then why would I not want to live my life exemplifying His mission the same way? It wasn't until I was fully convicted of what Jesus did by sacrificing for me that it finally clicked why He wants me to do the exact same thing to those around me. If we truly embody Christ, we should be driven to continuously hunger to become more like Christ.

Pushing Past Persecution

What about the times when you are in the middle of the fire? How do you handle it when the brutal persecution from your enemies looks like it's never going to cease? What do you do with thoughts of how much more rejection and pain you can handle? How do you take part in the act of biblically turning the other cheek?

"You have heard the law that says the punishment must match the injury: 'An eye for an eye, and a tooth for a tooth.' But I say, do not resist an evil person! If someone slaps you on the right cheek, offer the other cheek also. If you are sued in court and your shirt is taken from you, give your coat, too."

—Matt. 5:38–40

How?

When I really drew near to the Lord on my journey, there were times when I was very sensitive to hearing His call for acts of obedience He was leading me to do. Most of the time, I knew it was a conviction from the Lord because it was to do things I literally did not want to do as the healing person—things like swallowing every ounce of pride and being the bigger person. There were moments when the Lord would heavily place it on my heart to reach out to my husband or his family through an act of kindness, truth, or love. I invested so much into each and every thing that I sent or spoke. I'm talking about hours of prayer over what I wrote, prayers by my entire biblical community, and pouring out from the bottom of my heart in an overflow of unconditional love. It was everything I had—and it was *hard*.

My immediate responses to the Lord's calls were usually "Lord, please, no." He was constantly calling me out of my comfort zone. The hardest part for me was that I would humbly lay all I was out there and then usually be met with either painful rejection or dead silence. It was very difficult for me to not believe the lie that I was just humiliating myself because I never got to see what God was doing on the other side.

That's just it. You don't know what God is doing with it. You have to ask yourself this: Will I only choose to be kind and loving because I'm waiting or hoping for a positive response or result? If that's the case, then it's not sacrificial or genuine after all. Even if what you're called to do doesn't reveal any impact on others, your acts of obedience to God's call should be your ultimate driving factor and mission.

I had to condition myself to learn that you choose love because it's what Jesus would do. You fight to reconcile because it's what Jesus died for *us* to do. I had to continue to believe God would bless my love and acts of obedience, and that's all that mattered.

God sees everything. He sees the genuineness of your heart. But he also sees my enemies' hearts. If they are cold, ugly, or hateful to me, they will one day have to answer to the Lord for the way they treated me. I had to remember that my job was just to love, and God would deal with the pain inflicted on me. Any form of retaliation would completely negate my mission to look and become more like Him.

We bless those who curse us. We are patient with those who abuse us. We appeal gently when evil things are said about us.

—1 Cor. 4:12–13

There were times that people told me about incredibly hurtful things someone said about me. To be honest, I allowed it at times to strike me to my core. In the heat of those moments, I so badly wanted to throw in the towel and give up. It was in the fire that I had to remind myself that it's not the person; it's Satan, the real enemy, working against me. Satan knew exactly what I needed to hear to break me down and stop me from fighting, whether what they were saying was the truth or a complete lie. That's when you take it immediately to prayer.

"But I say, love your enemies! Pray for those who persecute you!"

—Matt. 5:44

You have to begin to condition yourself to separate the hate and the sin from the actual person. Hate the sin, not the person. Hating someone for hurting you only darkens you. You can't work through the healing process when you're bound by resentment. When you self-reflect on the fact that you, too, sin, hurt people, and make mistakes, you come to genuinely appreciate the power and meaning of grace. God sees and loves that person who is hurting you the same as He sees and loves you.

It's also imperative that you don't react negatively, because the truth is that gossip can be a total lie. You genuinely cannot prove someone said something hurtful about you if you didn't hear it directly from him or her. Even if you trust the messenger, don't fall into the trap of assuming the worst right away. Try your best to get rid of blame in the situation. It's so easy for words to be misunderstood, skewed, or stretched. There is also a possibility that there is a deeper intention than trying to hurt you. I came to learn over time that certain people told me certain things or exaggerated them in hopes it would trigger me to finally give in and hate my husband.

Yes, what is relayed to you really could be what was said, but that's not your burden to bear, regardless. Here's the thing. If it's actually not true, you just wasted your time dwelling on unnecessary hurt and ultimately let Satan win.

Only God knows what was actually said. Release it to the Lord and move forward, no matter how hard that may be.

Realize that your overall character and integrity will outweigh anything being poorly said about you, especially if it's not even close to the truth about who you are. Your actions, how you handle the situation, and how you don't allow it to define or destroy you will be the ultimate proof that their words can't win or even compete.

Instead of reacting negatively, pray for them and the situation so you can stay free. Honestly, my prayers initially started out very forced. In my times of self-pity and selfishness, they continued to be forced. But God knew exactly how to soften my heart. I would come to the end of myself by pleading for Him to help me love people even more and forgive them for what they had said or done and for the pain they were causing me. Over and over, God met me in those heartbreaking moments and gave me peace that only He can bring.

Prayer doesn't change the pain people cause you, but it frees you from holding on to bitterness and resentment that can only entangle you and distract you. Don't allow persecution to turn you away from your mission. Let it encourage you to fight that much harder because Satan clearly views you as a mighty threat. He only views you as a threat if he knows you're doing God's best.

People can only destroy you by the amount of power you give them. My friend, you have been given the greatest power, and that is the word of God and the living God that is spiritually engraved inside of you. Nothing anyone could ever say about you to harm you changes the power of what the gospel says about you. I encourage you to boldly stand firm and face persecution with integrity, poise, and trust in the Lord. Trust that He will come through for you no matter the circumstances that lie before you.

Look at Jesus. People hated Him. They hated Him so much that they crucified Him. But He gladly took the cross because of love. That is why love is one of your greatest weapons. You love people because you know that God will carry you, transform you, and bring a radical countercultural testimony out of you. You're a living, breathing testimony that people can look at and say there's no denying that Jesus lives powerfully through you by what you've allowed Him to do within you. The love of God compensates for human hate. My friend, let your love do the same to glorify Him!

> *"If the world hates you, remember that it hated me first. The world would love you as one of its own if you belonged to it, but you are no longer part of the world. I chose you to come out of the world, so it hates you."*

> —John 15:18–19

Radical Love

I want to share something with you that I sent to my husband. The purpose of this is to vulnerably reveal to you the end result of how powerfully I allowed Christ to work through me. Looking back on this, I'm nothing short of amazed, because I only could have done this by Christ alone. There is absolutely no way these words could have had the utmost heartfelt and genuine meaning if they had come from the selfish, worldly version of me. I placed my trust in Christ to teach me to become love. I want to challenge you to read what I wrote to my husband and think about someone who has or continues to hurt you.

June 16, 2018

If Jesus can love me [and forgive me] through my baggage, pain, sin, hardened heart, you name it, you best believe I choose *His* way to *love* the same....I chose to love you despite you being the man who abandoned me. I chose to love you for the man you are and see past the lies, anger, disrespect, cruel words to know you're just desperately hurting for Jesus. I chose to champion you when people told me I "deserve better." I chose to beg people to see you as a child of God and not a man defined by his choices. I chose to because you're my husband, and you best believe as much as I wanted to be so incredibly angry at you, I chose to love you instead and die to self. I chose to follow Jesus. I chose these things because Jesus *chose me*. While I knew it would be the most difficult option, my crown in heaven would be waiting. I pray you find yourself on your knees wrapped in our precious Father's arms, *overwhelmed* with His *abundant love* for you as a child of God.

Now, I want you to insert a person's name in the blank for your specific circumstance. I know this may feel incredibly forced right now. Stay with me, okay? Trust that with patience, grace, and time, your heart will start to genuinely transform to mean it. In prayer, ask God to give you the heart to truly believe and exemplify it. He's going to do a mighty work in you; I just know it.

If Jesus can love me through my baggage, pain, sin, hardened heart, you name it, you best believe I choose *His* way to *love* _____ the same.

I choose to love you despite _____

_____.

I choose to love you for the person you are and see past the

_____

_____.

I choose to recognize that you're just desperately hurting for Jesus.

I choose to champion you when and if people tell me I deserve better.

I choose to encourage people to see you as a child of God and not a person defined by _____

_____.

I choose to because you're my brother/sister in Christ.

I choose to love you instead and die to self.

I choose to follow Jesus.

I will choose these things because Jesus *chose me.*

While I know it may be the most difficult option, my crown in heaven *will* be waiting. I pray, _____, that you will find yourself on your knees wrapped in our precious Father's arms, *overwhelmed* by His *abundant love* for you as a child of God.

Friends, join me in choosing radical Christ-like love. When we choose to love radically, we're declaring, "I now grant the power of Jesus to freely flow out of me."

I challenge you to see each and every person as a valued, cherished child of God. I challenge you to lay down selfishness and choose kingdom righteousness. I challenge you to believe in the power of sacrificial love—radically moving mountains and fiercely summoning the kingdom above. I challenge you to boldly approach the throne with palms open wide, pleading, "Lord, just let me love like Jesus Christ."

I pray that the Lord teaches you about a love that knows no bounds. About a love that can no longer deny that Jesus lives and breathes in each and every part of you. A love that boldly claims, "Jesus, I choose to follow and love you." A love that's faithful and will not cease against the utmost formidable fear. A love that fiercely breaks chains and chooses to say, "I see you for you and not by the sin that entangles you." A love that chooses to instead say, "You're clean and free, in Jesus's name." Desire an unconditional love that pursues to the darkest trenches and the eternal ends of the earth.

When you choose to love this way, freedom reigns and breaks every chain. Choosing love in the darkest and what appears to be the most hopeless place ultimately makes you succumb to the mighty power of God's unending mercy and grace.

Choose radical love. Then wait to see the blessings that will overflow from above.

And he said to David, "You are a better man than I am, for you have repaid me good for evil. Yes, you have been amazingly kind to me today, for when the LORD put me in a place where you could have killed me, you didn't do it. Who else would let his enemy get away when he had him in his power? May the LORD reward you well for the kindness you have shown me today."

—1 Sam. 24:17–19

Make allowance for each other's faults, and forgive anyone who offends you. Remember, the LORD forgave you, so you must forgive others. Above all, clothe yourselves with love, which binds us all together in perfect harmony. And let the peace that comes from Christ rule in your hearts. For as members of one body you are called to live in peace.

—Col. 3:13–15

Chapter 4

Full Armor

For some women, putting on their favorite pair of heels makes them feel like they could conquer the world. For men, maybe it's their favorite sleek suit.

You feel empowered. You feel classy. You feel unstoppable.

That is, you feel that way until time passes and your feet start bearing the pain or you start to feel stiff and sweaty in that suit. At some point, you're desperately longing for a break, and you end up feeling complete relief to just take off those heels or that suit coat. While they looked beautiful and felt empowering in the moment, the feeling ended up being temporary and exhausting.

The world tells us to dress in complete confidence in ourselves because we can become our own success, which supposedly leads to nothing but happiness. The world tells us to dress to intimidate so we can get our way. The world tells us to dress in nothing but name brands to boast that our status is greater than the other person's.

If what the world is telling us to dress in is actually the truth, why do we keep coming back for more?

Why are we never fully satisfied?

Why does it always end up making us feel incomplete?

It's interesting how the choices we make to clothe ourselves can impact the steps we take. We're either walking
into bondage or walking into freedom. I don't know about
you, but I want freedom. When we clothe ourselves with the
things of the world, we only end up depleted because those
things are nothing but fleeting.

Imagine, then, the magnitude of power you embody by
putting on the full armor of God. Your feet are completely
protected and can freely walk in gospel peace. Your belt is
embellished with the most powerful truth—the word of God.
Your heart is guarded by kingdom righteousness. From head
to toe, you're flawlessly covered in a mighty salvation. In your
very hands lies the power of the spirit to conquer all things
with Christ. You will never tire because your God is your
strength and mighty fortress. He never ceases to fight and
go before you.

Choose strength. Choose dignity. Choose humility.
Choose confidence in the word of God. Choose Jesus. I can
affirm that you will never tire of wearing these things, and
they sure look good on everyone. Now let's put on the full
armor of God.

*Therefore, put on every piece of God's armor so you will be able
to resist the enemy in the time of evil. Then after the battle you
will still be standing firm.*

—Eph. 6:13

Shield of Faith

On **July 2, 2018**, I was almost killed in a car accident. That particular evening, I was driving to the place I always go to have quiet time with the Lord for my really big heart-to-heart moments. On my way there, the song "All In" by Matthew West came on the radio. Looking to my left, everything was completely clear, so I started to pull out to get across the main road.

Again, I looked to my left when I was almost to the median, and out of nowhere, a car came flying at supernatural speed toward my driver's side. It was about an arm's length from my door, and that moment, I was convinced I was about to die. I gripped my steering wheel for dear life, praying that somehow I would miss the impact. Then the driver collided with my car, and I felt the entire car lift up. Immediately, I looked back to see the damage, since miraculously he hadn't hit me directly. My dogs were in the back, and not even one of their hairs was touched.

I jumped out of the car to look for the driver, only to see a man running over to me. He had witnessed the entire thing and memorized the other driver's license plate as he left the scene. Yes, it was a hit and run. Another man turned his car around to tell me he witnessed the driver recklessly flying down the road without his lights on. How thankful I was that God gave me guardian angels that day. I know without a doubt that Satan wanted to take me out, but my God is greater.

It's important that I share with you what happened earlier that day. My mentor, Tammy, called me and told me it was imperative that she share something with me. She then told me that her sister felt heavily on her heart that I needed

Psalm 23:4 prayed over me and that I needed to pray it over myself as well.

> *Even though I walk through the valley of the shadow of death,*
> *I will fear no evil,*
> *for you are with me;*
> *your rod and your staff,*
> *they comfort me.*

—Ps. 23:4 ESV

After the accident, I called Tammy and told her what had happened. We walked through the scripture she had sent me earlier. The shadow of death literally was that car. It was dark out, and the driver did not have his headlights on, which is why I didn't see him until he was right next to me. Yet God was with me; I was faithfully reminded of that looking back earlier that day. The Lord used two of my prayer warriors as intercessors to pray a hedge of protection over me. None of us were aware of what was going to come up against me, but God had spiritually and physically covered me.

Now every time I hear that song, I'm reminded of my accident. What I love about God being in the details of playing that song is that I can always trust going straight into the depths with God. I can say that in full confidence because of the truth that fear cannot hold us down since He conquered the grave. I was equipped with a literal shield of armor that day, protected in a mighty way. The only damage I had was an almost-totaled car, a busted-open knee, a mild concussion, and torn ligaments in my neck that would require three months of extensive therapy. But in retrospect, the accident could have cost my life.

God has the power to shield you from the enemy, especially when it's completely out of your control. So you walk, and you fear no evil, for your God is with you. Nothing—not anything beyond your imagination—can ever stand against you.

> *"The thief's purpose is to steal and kill and destroy. My purpose is to give them a rich and satisfying life."*
>
> —John 10:10

Spiritual Warfare

The Lord declares each and every one of us His precious children with a divine purpose. With purpose comes power, and Satan despises that. Just as God has a set mission for us, Satan has an alternative agenda. If we think the enemy isn't real and downplay that he's prowling around waiting for his opportunity to attack, we're completely deceived. You will be substantially ill-equipped because you can't combat or resist something if you don't think it truly exists.

> *Stay alert! Watch out for your great enemy, the devil. He prowls around like a roaring lion, looking for someone to devour. Stand firm against him, and be strong in your faith. Remember that your family of believers all over the world is going through the same kind of suffering you are.*
>
> —1 Pet. 5:8–9

Before enduring this journey, I did not understand spiritual warfare at all. It wasn't until I really dived in deeply with my counselor, Wendy, and my mentor, Tammy, that I began to understand how important it is to maintain a state of awareness that Satan is always ready to attack.

Catch all the foxes,
those little foxes,
before they ruin the vineyard of love,
for the grapevines are blossoming!

—Song of Sol. 2:15

Foxes are notorious for being sneaky. You know who else is? Satan. One by one, foxes sneak into our vineyards that are blooming with our mission, our ministry, and our blessings because we're not keeping watch. If we're not keeping watch, should we be surprised to look back at the destruction that happened before our very eyes?

That's how the enemy works. He doesn't always drop the big bombs on you but slowly creeps in until the cracks under your feet crumble the ground beneath you. That is especially true when you're fighting fiercely for God's kingdom. Think about it. If Satan already has you trapped in his lies and temptations, he doesn't have to work that hard to keep you there; reality is, you aren't much of a threat to him. Doing kingdom work, on the other hand, infuriates him and sets him on a mission to *attempt* to destroy God's plan.

At first, this sounded really discouraging to me. If knowing spiritual attacks may increase because I'm doing more for the Lord, should that really ignite a fight in me? Not only was I fighting for my mission and myself, but I was also interceding on my husband's behalf by praying over the biblical provision God wanted to fulfill for him. I remember telling Wendy, "This already sounds defeating. I can't imagine thinking so many more battles potentially lie ahead because of where God is calling me."

What I came to learn is that battles don't become more powerful; *you do*. Scripture doesn't say that at some point your troubles and battles in this world will stop because you are a believer. In fact, it promises that we will face them.

> *"I have told you all this so that you may have peace in me. Here on earth you will have many trials and sorrows. But take heart, because I have overcome the world."*

—John 16:33

You become more powerful because you clothe yourself with armor. The enemy has a harder time trying to attack and defeat you when you have an added layer of protection surrounding you.

Don't forget to keep tabs on your bases:

Where do you find yourself most vulnerable?

Is it when you're down physically, spiritually, emotionally, or mentally?

What attacks are you more prone to?

Self-worth? Purpose? Your past? Pains? Mistakes?

What things trigger you?

Temptations? Situations? People? Places?

My spiritual attacks were always based on my self-worth. I knew my times of vulnerability were in mentally or emotionally stressful situations. The place they were most prominent was work or, in general, wherever unexpected circumstances arose. If I started doubting myself, then the lies of worthlessness tagged right along. Once I knew how the enemy worked on me, I could immediately remind myself that it's just him trying to attack me, and the feeling was not rooted in truth.

If you start to feel overwhelmed with anxiety, doubt, fear, lies, or the temptation to give up, remember that those things are never rooted in or from the Lord. It's your job to fill yourself up with the truths that are from Him and of Him.

As you start to see these things creep in, I challenge you to remember God has overcome, and all you're called to do is to be ready—clothed in your armor. Now let's get equipped by firmly standing your ground on the word of God.

The Word of God

In moments when anxiety was overtaking me, the only thing I could control was prayer and reminding myself of God's truths by professing scripture. One of the most important skills you should equip yourself with is the ability to go straight to scripture when doubts, fears, and lies creep in. Satan wants you to buy into the lies that you're not worthy, you can't get through this, God has forsaken you, and you're just a fool for believing God will come through for you.

Your greatest weapon is the word of God. Nothing can come between you and this truth. His word pierces right through all Satan is trying to use to destroy you. Meditate and memorize scripture to help equip you spiritually so you can have verses on hand in time of need.

This is the scripture I always prayed over myself when I was under spiritual attack:

For God has not given us a spirit of fear and timidity, but of power, love, and self-discipline.

—2 Tim. 1:7

This scripture is so powerful because it covers all your bases. You have the ability through Christ to combat the fear that is trying to take you out. You are declared bold, not timid, because the Spirit of God lives in you. Love is a powerful gift because Christ died for it to conquer evil. Self-discipline is imperative to be steadfast in your faith.

Consistently begin to practice outwardly what you preach inwardly. Condition yourself to rely on scripture daily to help you fight your battles. Self-medicating with worldly things can never compare to the peace Christ brings.

There were also many nights I struggled to fall asleep. My mind would start to wander, convincing myself that fighting for my husband and my marriage was hopeless. I started to look up sermons and testimonies to listen to as I lay down to try to sleep. I was then able to find rest spiritually because of the truth spoken over me; I was also able to rest physically because I was equipped with promised gospel peace.

Find what methods work best for you.

For me, journaling became very beneficial and crucial. I could write out what my fears or doubts were and then search for scripture I could use to cover them. When they came up again, I had my references to turn to immediately. I also utilized sticky notes. As empowering scripture, songs, or words of wisdom came to me, I started writing them down and sticking them on my door, my mirror, and in my prayer closet. Every time I left my house, I saw Ephesians 6:13 on the front door. It reminded me to put on my full armor of God before I walked out. Every time I looked in a mirror, there was a sticky note that reflected God's truth.

At first it may feel like you're forcing yourself to have constant reminders, but this self-discipline starts transforming into a habit. Then the habit becomes an empowerment and a fierce weapon.

Whatever methods work best for you to stand firm in scripture, know that they will help equip you while you're in your deepest, darkest trenches and prepare you to fight against the world that is telling you to run. Let's get ready to dive into those trenches.

All Scripture is inspired by God and is useful to teach us what is true and to make us realize what is wrong in our lives. It corrects us when we are wrong and teaches us to do what is right. God uses it to prepare and equip his people to do every good work.

—2 Tim. 3:16–17

Chapter 5

The Trenches

The trenches. Deep. Dark. Dirty. When you're in the trenches, that means war. From surrendering to the Lord in the abandonment of your will and plans, to stripping yourself of pride in the humbling, to equipping yourself to love radically, and finally to powerfully clothing yourself with the full armor of God, you're now ready to enter the battlefield.

The entire gospel is a declaration of victory. To be victorious, there must first be a battle that has to take place. Without a battle, there would be no purpose for victory. If you reflect on some of the most triumphant people in the Bible, you recognize that they endured being beaten, burned, tortured, persecuted, and pushed to their furthest limits. Yet *they won.*

You too, friend, are going to be victorious. Right now, you might be fighting with all you have to believe it. You have to receive the truth that the battle you're facing doesn't even compare to the victory awaiting. Let's prepare for battle, get ready to stand in these trenches, look up filled with hope, and allow the Lord to conquer this war.

Calm before the Storm

Your battle is very real. Whether you feel it's big or small, it's still your battle to endure. When you're fully aware that the brutal force of the battle is coming but hasn't happened yet, what do you do? You probably anxiously wait for the moment that the first shots are fired. I've lived in this place many times. I knew the battle in my fight for my marriage had just begun, but I didn't know when or how the brunt of the forces would hit the hardest. All I knew was *it was coming.*

We have an awareness that being anxious about what is to come is never beneficial because anxiety doesn't actually change anything; it only leaves you unsettled and far from peace. But that doesn't make it any easier to completely release it.

This, friend, is where we cue the calm before the storm. The phrase *calm before the storm* has been defined by the *Cambridge Dictionary* as "a quiet or peaceful period before a period during which there is great activity, argument, or difficulty."

Let me take you back to the day the Lord taught me about the calm before the storm. On **April 22, 2018, at 3:30 p.m.**, I was just two months into my battle. I remember standing in my kitchen when the song "Psalm 46" by Shane & Shane came on my Pandora app on the TV. In that moment, I had an indescribable amount of chills that physically flooded my body. I just knew there was something about this song that the Lord needed me to hear.

Take out your Bible or whatever device you have and look up Psalm 46. This psalm is centered on the power of God, who can do all things—all things like calm the most powerful wind surges you could ever imagine. All things like

100 percent tame the massive chaos that reckless waves produce in the deepest sea.

Despite the chaos that may surround us, God tells us to remain in a place of stillness. When I first sat with this, I realized that we don't acknowledge just how powerful our hearts really are and can be. Our hearts need to be stilled because they can steer us in terrifying directions, give us anxiety and doubt, and also have the power to lead us into defying God.

"The human heart is the most deceitful of all things, and desperately wicked. Who really knows how bad it is?"

—Jer. 17:9

Our hearts at times may literally be stronger willed than the greatest battles, winds, or waves. We flood ourselves with panic and anxiety when we're in the trenches because we are desperately plotting how we can grasp some sort of control. God knows this. He's not surprised by it. Because He is fully aware of this, in His love and mercy, He wants to redirect us to the place of being still.

God knows He is the only thing powerful enough to take hold of your heart. His purpose for you is to be still and calm before the brunt of the storm. If we choose to defy Him before the storm, why would we end up choosing to submit and trust Him once it actually hits? You have to recognize how important it is to build your trust in the Lord as you wait. It's so important because you need that trust and a genuine belief in His promises to cling to as the battle starts to grow.

God knows that no amount of worry or anticipation will change your outcome because He's already gone before you and won this thing. Scripture never says that you are to figure it out or fight it on your own.

"The LORD will fight for you; you need only to be still."

—Exod. 14:14 NIV

Lay down your anticipation of fear of the battle before you; instead, choose to be still and wait on the Lord. He will make your heart still if you let Him. In being still, we are met with peace. Remember, you have the full capability to put on your very important piece of armor—the shoes of the gospel of peace. This is the time to do it. Being still means you confidently trust whatever direction the unknown battle is about to go, and that will ultimately bring Him glory. You, my friend, should proudly declare, "My God is for me; therefore, this battle can never destroy me."

"Be still, and know that I am God!"

—Ps. 46:10

Better Is One Day in Your Courts

Choosing to stand for Christ is considered incredibly countercultural. Our world tells us that if it's difficult, go find another alternative that's easy. Go self-medicate with alcohol, drugs, addictions, idols, or materialism. Instead, we should be spurred on to be a people who say go *heal yourself* in Christ alone.

One of the most challenging encounters I faced in standing firm against adversity was on **May 22, 2018.** That was the day I went to court to fight for the reconciliation of my marriage. My warriors were rallied and lifted me up with powerful prayer. I needed a miracle's worth of strength to give me courage to stand before the judge that day.

> *A single day in your courts*
> *is better than a thousand anywhere else!*
> *I would rather be a gatekeeper in the house of my God*
> *than live the good life in the homes of the wicked.*
>
> —Ps. 84:10

As I prepared, I kept fervently praying and reminding myself of this scripture. I was fighting in desperation by convincing myself that this day would boldly proclaim this living truth. Have you had a moment like this—being faced point-blank with the choice of bowing down in fear to please a person or to stand boldly against the odds for your faith in God? This was definitely one of those encounters that significantly tested the genuineness of my faith.

> *These trials will show that your faith is genuine. It is being tested as fire tests and purifies gold—though your faith is far more precious than mere gold. So when your faith remains strong through many trials, it will bring you much praise and glory and honor on the day when Jesus Christ is revealed to the whole world.*
>
> —1 Pet. 1:7

I was so thankful to have two of my toughest prayer warriors, Montoya and Shannon, with me that day. It was powerful because they, too, had the opportunity to share the gospel boldly alongside me. Before we entered the courtroom, we gathered in prayer, fully expectant that God was going to show up in a mighty way to do what He said He would do. People around us were staring, some in utter confusion about why we were praying in front of the courtroom. More than anything, that simple moment invigorated my confidence because people got to witness our dependence and belief in Jesus. They witnessed the power we proclaimed and felt confident in by inviting the Holy Spirit to be with us in our battle.

As we entered the courtroom, immediately I could feel an evil presence flooding the room. I cannot even begin to explain how eerie it was—massive chills and an overwhelming feeling of pure darkness. In that moment, I knew in my spirit that the judge did not know the Lord. I truly believe it was the Holy Spirit warning me. Right away, I opened my Bible to Ephesians 6 and pleaded for God to equip me with the full armor of God since this was about to be one brutal battle.

When I say the Lord never steered me wrong once, I mean it. I'll tell you why. I approached the stand to testify, extremely terrified and clutching my Bible against my chest for dear life. The opposing attorney asked me, "Why do you believe in reconciliation?" Before I answered, I prayed, "Lord, let it be Your words, not mine," and then I said, "Because I believe in Jesus. It's the purpose of His ministry." The judge, without hesitation, actually scoffed and rolled his eyes at me when I mentioned the name of Jesus. Was the Holy Spirit on point or what? Instantly, I knew that reconciliation was absolutely not going to be granted to me. I knew that in less than five minutes of that hearing. You may initially assume that I felt completely defeated, but it actually spurred on this insane amount of passion to fight for my faith, my belief, and my high King. That kind of power could only have been spurred on in me because Jesus was there, ready to show up and do a mighty work through me.

I made my choice. I chose to stand for the Lord and fight to honor what God's word states about the ministry of reconciliation and the power He has to redeem. It's the entire ministry of the gospel. Think about all He has done for us. He's redeemed and reconciled each and every one of us lost sheep back to His loving arms; that's the bold and honest truth. We are called as His servants to do so, too. So, friends, I confidently sat there, spoke the truth of the gospel, and did it with a smile on my face. I saw this encounter in a brand new positive light; here I was, granted an opportunity to stand for Jesus's name!

As the hearing was coming to an end, I continued to fixate on my Bible and trust that God's hand was in this. While I was praying, my attorney tapped my hand and pointed to his notes with his pencil. He had drawn a cross. In my heart, I knew he was led to do it to encourage me and remind me that this is why I had fought and why I would continue to fight—for the cross. Even in the smallest details, God faithfully shows up in reminders like this that He is there, and He gives us faithful warriors to fight alongside us so we don't have to go through it alone.

The judge did not grant reconciliation, which, as I shared, was no surprise. But did I ever walk out of that courtroom with a completely different and empowering prize! I was gifted immaculate, unsurpassable peace that flooded over me and through me. I had peace knowing that I was obedient to God's word and had honored my vows by standing for my marriage. From this experience, I learned that even if it's not the outcome you thought was best, God will honor you by giving you His best because of your surrender and obedience.

With Christ, no matter the trenches we find ourselves in or the courts we may stand up against, we are always declared victorious.

"Blessed is anyone who does not stumble on account of me."

—Matt. 11:6 NIV

Ready to Give Up the Fight

It was **June 12, 2018, at 3:35 a.m.** Would you believe me if I told you that on this very date, it was the second and last time throughout my entire journey that I was infuriatingly angry? As I am writing this, I am again in so much awe at the transformative power of God to radically change bitter and broken hearts. I remember sitting on the floor frustrated. Angry. Enraged. Questioning God's goodness. I even indulged in a dose of self-pity, pleading, "God, why me?" and "God, just take this from me!" The weight of the battle kept driving me deeper into what felt like sinking sand.

I kept fighting but not seeing.

I kept believing but not receiving.

I kept praying, but it was silent.

It didn't make sense, and I honestly told God, "I just don't want any part of it anymore. I'm done." In that moment, I stormed to my bedroom, livid beyond belief, and dug out my ring box from the closet. I took off my rings, put them in the perfectly stitched leather box that should have never needed to be opened again, and threw the box as forcefully as I could at the wall. In that moment, I was so heartbroken and a hopeless wreck. Obviously, I didn't think that decision through all the way because the box broke, and my rings went flying all over the place. There I was, sobbing uncontrollably, still telling God, "I'm done! I'm done!" At the same time, I was anxiously searching the floor to find those rings.

Think back to a time when you told God, "I'm done!" Have you? Are you ready to?

Maybe as you're reading this, you're actively living out the words in utter defeat. There's not an ounce left in you to convince you to keep going. But, friend, bear with me. On my journey, in my greatest times of desperation, sorrow, and excruciating pain and defeat, I can vividly tell you that those were the times God powerfully met me.

This moment, surely, was one of those.

As I was searching for my rings under my nightstand, I came across one of my Bibles on the floor. It just so happened to have a piece of paper very clearly sticking out of the pages. I begrudgingly pulled out the Bible and took out the paper. It was a note from my husband. It said, "**I will fight for you until my last breath. I love you.**"

If you thought I was enraged before, this moment only heightened every single emotion I was encountering. "Are you kidding me, God? Why would You show me this note when clearly it's nothing but a lie? If he loved me, he wouldn't have abandoned me. If he fought for me, there would be redemption. No, there's none of that here, but thanks for rubbing it in." That, in all transparency, was the ugly truth of the words that came out of me. I was real with God.

I share this encounter with you because I fully recognize that it's okay to have moments when you can't do it any longer. It's okay to be exhausted. But in the end, it comes down to accepting the fact that there will be times of being dirty. I'm talking a face fully submerged in mud—dirty, in the trenches. Stay with me. Take a deep breath. Fight through the anger, pain, and doubt, and instead, tell God, "I want to believe Your promises are true." Humbly cry and admit, "But God, I literally cannot do this without You." Suffering was never intended to punish you; God in His mercy will use it to stir up a revival in you.

> *We were crushed and overwhelmed beyond our ability to endure, and we thought we would never live through it. In fact, we expected to die. But as a result, we stopped relying on ourselves and learned to rely only on God, who raises the dead. And he did rescue us from mortal danger, and he will rescue us again. We have placed our confidence in him, and he will continue to rescue us. And you are helping us by praying for us. Then many people will give thanks because God has graciously answered so many prayers for our safety.*
>
> —2 Cor. 1:8–11

Sometimes, you may not have an immediate revelation or understanding of what God is trying to tell you in the midst of the trenches. For me, in the moment I just shared, I sure had no idea what God was trying to tell me by allowing me to see that note. All I knew in the moment was that God provided a small, yet very clear reminder to keep going. Needless to say, I put my rings back on and knew God was telling me I was going to be okay. God was clearly in this, and He wasn't going to let go of me.

Right now, you may be feeling that way about a current situation. Or it might even be about one from the past that you are still struggling to comprehend and grasp what the purpose may be. Job is one of the perfect examples to relate to in the midst of battles and sufferings. In Job 42, scripture reveals that God faithfully brought Job comfort and reassurance even when he didn't understand the strife he had to endure. Job was flooded with doubt, fear, and uncertainty. But his feelings toward God never changed who God was or what He would or could do.

Fast-forward to **December 24, 2018**. I'm sitting on the couch, typing up journal entries into my book's outline, simply going through the motions, and it suddenly hit me. I was massively flooded with the understanding of why I had to be in that dark place in that moment.

It was never about the note specifically being from my husband. It was God all along trying to tell me something.

I will fight for you until my last breath. I love you.

Do you know who fought for me until His last breath? **Jesus.**

Do you know why He did? Because **He loves me.**

It's a promise, a declaration, so great that we get to cherish it for eternity because of what He did for you and me.

Looking back, this message was designed to serve as a reminder. It was a reminder that Jesus never gave up on me. In my darkest moments, He has always been there. My feelings and doubts never altered the power of the truth that Jesus was 100 percent with me even when I couldn't see it. Friend, he isn't giving up on you, either. Keep pushing through.

The Long Way Home

One of the greatest battles within the battle itself is usually the amount of time it takes to overcome it. I found myself easily frustrated with the thought of this never-ending battle. If God was almighty, powerful, and could do the impossible, why wouldn't He just take this battle from me now? I wrestled with that a lot. My *now* was, of course, the best timing; I wasn't sure why God didn't see that, too. When I reflect back on my journal entries, I can't help but laugh when I was only three months in and felt this battle was taking forever. If I had to tell myself then that I had another five months to go, I absolutely would have said, "No way! No!" When I received my abandonment letter, I thought I legally had only 60 days to fight, but it turned into a solid 229.

That's the thing about God; it's all in His time. Most often, His time tends to be the long way home. There absolutely are times that battles are conquered much more quickly than we could ever ask God for. How I want to encourage you in this is that your long way home doesn't go without purpose or value.

The Lord took hold of me, and I was carried away by the Spirit of the Lord to a valley filled with bones. He led me all around among the bones that covered the valley floor. They were scattered everywhere across the ground and were completely dried out. Then he said to me, "Speak a prophetic message to these bones and say, 'Dry bones, listen to the word of the Lord! This is what the Sovereign Lord says: Look! I am going to put breath into you and make you live again! I will put flesh and muscles on you and cover you with skin. I will put breath into you, and you will come to life. Then you will know that I am the Lord.'"

—Ezek. 37:1–2, 4–6

According to this passage in scripture, the bones came to life, not in one piece but piece by piece. This passage teaches us an important message. Every step in the process is important and matters. God brought the bones to life in phases because He is a God of details. God believed that each step was worth investing and spending time on to show Ezekiel the intricacy, beauty, and power God could bring. Ezekiel witnessed that God could bring even the darkest sight of death back to life. It was with each step that Ezekiel had to choose whether to continue to be obedient and believe that God was going to bring this prophecy to life.

Another passage in scripture that really challenged my heart to appreciate enduring a long journey is in Exodus.

When Pharaoh finally let the people go, God did not lead them along the main road that runs through Philistine territory, even though that was the shortest route to the Promised Land. God said, "If the people are faced with a battle, they might change their minds and return to Egypt." So God led them in a round-about way through the wilderness toward the Red Sea. Thus the Israelites left Egypt like an army ready for battle.

—Exod. 13:17–18

I want to emphasize that God knows there is always a quick alternative to each of our battles. It's no surprise to Him, and He easily could make that happen for you and me. As you see in the above scripture, God's heart is revealed behind His decision to lead the Israelites the long way home; it was to protect them from returning to destruction. If God were to give us our way and show us the easy way out, our hearts wouldn't be spiritually challenged to desire God's best for us. It would completely negate any room for growth or opportunity to lean into Him and trust Him wholeheartedly.

Over time, I genuinely grew to appreciate the long journey the Lord took me on because I wouldn't have been able to write half of this book without it. Each day played a significant role in making me the woman of God I can firmly stand tall as today. He's doing the exact same thing for you, too. When we transform our thoughts to long for what God is trying to teach us in the battle, we expectantly wait for the victory that lies just outside the trenches. The amount of time will not change the fact that the outcome will always be victory.

Ray of Hope

On **December 11, 2018**, I was walking my dogs, and the weather outside was on the brink of a storm. It was early afternoon, but I could have been convinced it was near dusk by the darkness that disseminated across the entire sky.

Despite the consuming, thick, heavy darkness, there was still enough light to see around me. The darkness and the emerging storm couldn't overpower the light because the sun was still shining above the clouds. Although it may not have been as bright out because the clouds masked the sun, the storm would at some point pass, and the sun would shine again. When the clouds slowly begin to part, the sun starts to break through. Sometimes, it starts only as a single ray. One by one, the rays stretch far out across the sky to remind you that hope is rising, the light is coming. When the sun breaks through, it becomes so blinding and powerful that you forget the surrounding clouds even exist.

Your storm may be clouding your ray of hope, but remember, it doesn't change the fact that the Lord is always with you. He's still there, watching over you from above your clouds, longing for the right moment to pry open the sky and bring you your silver lining. Fight through the clouds and patiently wait for your storm to pass.

In my times of doubt, my best friend, Montoya, always used to tell me, "Your rainbow is coming." She was always so faithful, pushing me to cling to hope and reminding me that the beauty to come out of my battle was just on the horizon.

If I quit too soon, I'd miss my rainbow. Friends, I hope you don't miss out on your rainbow.

I did some research on rainbows and came across an interesting article.

> According to the Bible, the rainbow is the sign of God's promise to mankind that he will never again flood the Earth. Indeed, rainbows often indicate that the rain has passed. Generally, it will be sunny when you see a rainbow, but rain clouds...will be just a short distance away....Rainbows are frequently seen in the wake of a rainstorm. **They come when the sunlight breaks through rain clouds** (emphasis added).[1]

One day I was driving to church in the middle of a massive storm, and ironically, the song "Praise You in This Storm" by Casting Crowns came on the radio. When I finally pulled into a parking spot, I glanced over my shoulder and saw the most breathtaking, beautiful rainbow radiating across the sky. I was met with such solitude and was simply reminded that rainbows come *after* the storm.

When the clouds feel so heavy that you start believing the lie that they'll never lift, look up to the sky and envision His promises. He will rebuild what was ruined, and He will restore all that was lost. Your rainbow is coming.

"The fields that used to lie empty and desolate in plain view of everyone will again be farmed. And when I bring you back, people will say, 'This former wasteland is now like the Garden of Eden! The abandoned and ruined cities now have strong walls

1. Joe Rao, "Rainbows: How They Form & How to See Them," March 15, 2011, LiveScience, https://www.livescience.com/30235-rainbows-formation-explainer.html.

*and are filled with people!' Then the surrounding nations that
survive will know that I, the LORD, have rebuilt the ruins and
replanted the wasteland."*

—Ezek. 36:34–36

Our sorrows and trials all serve a purpose. We serve a
sovereign God. Shift your perspective, and instead of "Why
me?" say, "God, show me." Ask Him what He is trying to
teach or show you in this time or season. You can rest assured
that your battle will have an end at some point. Until then,
realize and acknowledge that it won't be complete until God
has gotten *His* end in what He desires for each of us to gain
and understand—ultimately for our healing and for His glory.

**The choice is in your own hands. Will you bow down
to fear and the adversity that appears to be debilitating on
every end, or will you trust God and stand to fight?**

When you're in the trenches, there's nowhere else to look
but up. So look up in hope, adoration, and full expectation
that God is going to move and do exactly what He said He
will do. Don't give up your fight. The battle may appear
formidable, but you have the fiercest God who already has
gone ahead of you. Stand firm in the trenches, remain fully
equipped in your armor, and get ready to be faithful and fight
the good fight of faith. Your Savior is coming for you, and
the victory is yours.

But the Lord stands beside me like a great warrior.
Before him my persecutors will stumble.
They cannot defeat me.

—Jer. 20:11

Chapter 6

Strength in Numbers

Driving in the middle of severe thunderstorms is one of my greatest fears. The storms beat down with gargantuan force, blinding the couple of feet before me. Angst arises, adrenaline kicks in, and now I'm fully aware I have little to no control and can only go incredibly slowly. I desperately grasp a glimpse of light from the cars ahead of me—that is, if there are any. The moment I begin to recognize I'm surrounded by other cars ahead, behind, and next to me, my body immediately floods with overwhelming peace. I'm no longer alone. Hazard lights begin to come on to communicate the danger that lies ahead if I don't yield to caution.

How much do these cars symbolize what biblical community does for us in the midst of our own storms? In debilitating winds, a band of brothers and sisters stands to fight against the resistance. In the downpour of tears and suffering, there is a shielding umbrella of spoken truth to keep you from drowning. The light each person radiates fills you with hope that this darkness, too, shall pass. Accountability is the warning spoken in truth and in love that not only helps you overcome the storm but also conquer it.

I couldn't even fathom walking through my storm without the community that flooded around me, kept me afloat, and physically carried me. In my weakest moments, I trusted in my community and my bond with these people to remind me of the promises of God when I believed the lie that He had forsaken me.

I desperately pleaded for accountability to become the woman of God that scripture calls me to be. People kept me on track to stay on my mission; they never allowed me to veer off course, even though it was so much easier to throw my hands up, quit, and run. The one who stands firm doesn't stand firm alone. The toughest battles call for the toughest warriors.

In the process, you may lose the unsteady ones along the way, ones who turn to worldly wisdom and self-gratification instead of godly wisdom. You have to make the sacrifice to choose your warriors wisely because it can make or break your ability to fight in the battle.

In the end, you see that those who are rooted in faith are devoted to walking alongside you through trial by nothing but truth. They have a vision of what lies ahead, and that vision is the fulfillment of the promises of God, no matter how impossible things may also appear before them. They, too, are equipped in the toughest armor—the word of God.

With these people as your community, nothing can stand against you. These people are the backbone and the reason I can stand as tall as I do today. The beauty of community is that you're gifted with a piece of each person that pours into you. It's those pieces that God places intricately together into the final product He is continuously molding in you.

Bad Company

The world promises fulfillment by enticement into sin. To be satisfied, you have to "do you," as society says, and not worry about anyone else around you. Your circle will either draw you to become more holy or entrap you in the never-ending bondage of sin. If you aren't held accountable by faithful believers, how reliable is your true awareness when you begin to stray?

Our hearts cannot be trusted because emotions are fleeting and oftentimes incredibly deceiving. We tend to do what we feel is best, not what the Bible says is best. You will never find freedom by trapping yourself in sin and toxic friend circles. Friendships in your life should be life-giving, not life-depleting. You even have to be careful with believers in your circle. It's easy for someone to claim they love Jesus, but a true testament of their genuine conviction and love for the Lord is measured by their actions and the fruit they bear.

As a face is reflected in water,
  so the heart reflects the real person.

—Prov. 27:19

I've been told by some past friends, "God *just* wants you to be happy, so you do what makes you happy." **That is completely unbiblical.** There are no verses in the Bible that ever state to follow your heart and take part in what you deem is best because it's all about your happiness. It's honestly just another way of saying to go ahead and be selfish; it'll be okay because God loves you anyway, and if you're happy with your choices or sins, then God will be happy for you, too.

You shouldn't be driven by what makes you *happy* but rather by what makes you *holy*. Holiness may not be the most appealing route, but it's the **most promising route.** Genuine joy finds contentment in *all* situations. That means in the brunt of the storm, in suffering, or in the unsurpassable peace in the calm.

Your friends' love for you shouldn't be placed in a box. A good check to evaluate the relationships you have is by this scripture:

Rejoice with those who rejoice; mourn with those who mourn.

—Rom. 12:15 NIV

If people are only supporting you in the highs but leaving you dry and alone in the lows, then those people genuinely do *not* have your best interest at heart. I had to make a lot of difficult decisions in slowly releasing friendships while I was mid-battle on my journey. I needed to be supported and surrounded by people who would stand and fight with me and push me to look more like Christ, not deny biblical truth or tell me what the flesh in me wanted to hear.

If I had held on to the ones who encouraged me to "just do you," I would have completely ventured off course from what the Lord had called me to do. It's in the weak moments when you're tempted to give up that you need your strong army to back you up.

There have also been circumstances in which I've wrestled with whether to hold on to certain relationships since it could be an opportunity for the Lord to use me as a light, someone they may not have had exposure to otherwise. If you struggle with those friendships, I encourage you to really pray through what the Lord could be using you for. If it continues to become a toxic cycle that only ends up draining you, it might be good to ask Him if it's time to release them.

If sinners entice you,
turn your back on them!

...don't go along with them!
  Stay far away from their paths.

—Prov. 1:10, 15

Convinced, Not Convicted

Let me tell you about my best friend, Montoya. That woman knows how to convict me like no other. She constantly challenges me and won't even allow me a split second to come close to doubting God. I will never forget the boldest thing she ever told me in the very beginning of my journey.

You're convinced, not convicted.

I developed a love-hate relationship with conviction. At first, I felt really offended by that, but honestly, she was right. I was convinced that I knew who God was and what He was supposed to be capable of, but I wasn't convicted because I wasn't faithfully living out what I claimed to be convinced of. My doubts were greater than my God. I could say the right things to myself, but until I actually believed them, my life wouldn't prove I actually trusted God. Montoya in her boldness had no problem calling me out on it.

Anytime I came to her expressing even the most miniscule ounce of doubt, she'd catch me and say her signature statement: "Rhianna, stop doubting and believe. God always goes for his sheep. **Don't doubt God!**" In her friendship, she was simply a testament to why I couldn't and shouldn't doubt God. She faithfully remained patient with me and never let me give up on my faith in God.

I was faced with yet another one of my most convicting conversations when I was having lunch one day with Becky, one of my mentors. She asked me if I would view this journey differently if my divorce went through, in spite of my fight and hope for reconciliation. My immediate response was, "I haven't really thought about it since all I've done is cling to hope for restoration." She challenged me to really draw near to the Lord.

Once she left, I sat with the Lord in quiet time, dissecting my thoughts about that question. Would it be different? It was in that moment that the Holy Spirit met me with the honest realization that more than likely my journey was going to end in divorce despite the fact that He was still calling me to fight. From that conversation forward, I took on an entirely new perspective.

Really think about this:

How much easier is it to fight for something with the hope of the outcome you personally are desiring for yourself versus fighting for something with astounding awareness it is going to end completely the opposite?

I had my answer to her question; I decided I was going to be the story that stood faithful to the end despite the outcome. It was what I was called to. But because I knew it was what I was called to do, did that make it any easier for me? Absolutely not! But my faithful community and my God sure did.

You Never Know Who You May Bless in the Process

ReEngage is one of the ministries I will forever be grateful to during my journey. It's a ministry founded by Watermark designed to empower you to fight for the godly marriage God ordained for you to have. **April 4, 2018,** two months into my journey, I showed up at ReEngage, desperately grasping for a ray of hope. The first testimony I heard reaffirmed I was called to take part in this ministry. The power and healing

God had done and was continuing to do in so many marriages was beyond encouraging.

Because of my experience, I want to encourage you to find your own place in a ministry community. It's so important to seek out a ministry you can specifically pour yourself into and where you can share whatever you're going through. In this, you continue to find not only hope and healing, but you will commune with people who may be able to relate to you through their own stories and the road they, too, have walked.

ReEngage taught me that healing has to start with *one person*. I faithfully made the choice and declaration that I was going to be that person.

Whatever your circumstance or story, know that you, too, have the power and the ability to be that one person.

One evening, I had the courage to attend what they called open group for the first time. In open group, they discussed the testimony or teaching for the night and then reflected on what role each person has played or could play in their own marriage testimony. I kept having this strong urge in my heart that I had to share my testimony without question. My entire being was trembling in fear and discouragement since I was the only one without a spouse in the room. There were at least 20 couples in the room.

This particular open group had leaders who encouraged everyone to go around in a circle and share a bit of their stories and why they had chosen to come to ReEngage. Most of the time, it's voluntary, but this was my night because I didn't really have the choice. As my turn drew closer and closer, I kept praying, "Lord, please give me strength to speak. I'm so terrified." My turn came, and I began to share my story. This was the first time I had publicly shared the battle I was facing outside of the direct people fighting alongside me in my friendships and community group. My voice began to quiver and tremble, and I completely broke down. In the moment, I felt so weak and ashamed as the only spouse completely alone. I couldn't even get through the beginning of my story without falling apart and losing it.

As I felt the agony and shame overcome me, I was met with arms that quickly wrapped around me without hesitation. One beautiful soul asked the entire room to bow and pray over me right away. Complete strangers. Pouring their hearts and love out in prayer. Washing my fears and doubts completely clean. In a moment of complete brokenness and convincing myself I was alone because my spouse wasn't present, I was immediately surrounded by my brothers and sisters in Christ who loved me without even knowing anything about me.

It was on this very night that I was blessed to meet some incredible people. Little did I know that these people would be a massive addition to my army of warriors who would fight alongside me until the very end. Oh, how they became some of my most faithful prayer warriors. As the night came to an end, multiple couples approached me and said they saw so much hope and courage in me that it gave them a stronger will to fight for their own marriage because I was doing it for the both of us—alone.

While I had shown up at this ministry looking for hope, I was also able to give unto others the exact same thing. From that moment forth, I chose to boldly keep showing up to that ministry. I was going to use the opportunity God had placed right in front of me. I decided I would stand for my marriage, learn how to become the most impeccable, godly wife through wisdom, further challenge myself in what it means to deny self and strip off pride, and encourage others to fight along the way.

A month later, **May 9, 2018**, the couple leading my open group was one of the couples whose testimonies had inspired me so much during this fight. I felt led to share a small bit of my testimony that I was, at the time, now going on three months, fighting for the marriage alone. Afterward, a man sitting next to me was tearing up as he approached me. With weary, worn eyes, he humbly looked at me and said I was his answered prayer for hope that night and that he had almost turned around three times before coming. He said he had contemplated the purpose of even showing up since he, too, was trying to begin his journey to fight and stand for his marriage alone.

If I hadn't followed the Lord's press on my heart to share my story, this man wouldn't have had the answer to his prayer and known why he needed to be there. The words spoken and the journey the Lord had given me in turn gave this man hope. What faithful lessons I learned that you genuinely never know the depth of whom you have the ability to bless along the way. It is simply by your trust and your obedience to the Lord.

Remember this, it's ultimately not about you. It's about what Jesus wants to do in you and *through* you.

Answered Prayers

Answered prayers—they give you the most incredible feeling, don't they? Sometimes they may not be what you expected or hoped for, but oh, how I love that the Lord in His goodness gives us exceedingly more.

My faithful prayer warriors on my journey were so many answered prayers in themselves that I'd probably have to write another book just to tell you about all of them. What I cherished so much about these beautiful people praying for me was that the Lord started binding us in such a deep way. We were spiritually becoming connected. As they were praying for me, they opened up their hearts and ears to the Lord and were able to respond to His leading because they had drawn near as they were interceding.

When I had my deepest breakdowns, my prayer warriors were usually the ones to meet me in those exact moments because the Lord told them to. God used them in ways they didn't realize at the time, which is what actually kept me going.

I knew God perfectly ordained these encounters to come together to remind me that the fight was not my own. Biblically, there was a purpose and a call for me to find rest because my God and my prayer warriors were praying and fighting for me.

May 12, 2018, served as one of my most significant moments in which God actually used multiple prayer warriors to unite with me all in one day. That day, my family and I were celebrating my sister's college graduation. We had a ton of people over, and I became overwhelmed with anxiety and pain since everyone kept asking me where my husband was and if he was coming. I got to the point where I couldn't fight back my emerging flood of tears with a forced, fake smile and ran off to my mom's closet and completely lost it.

I remember telling God that He was torturing me by telling me I had to keep fighting. In my arrogance, I told God this was the day I would finally be done and there was nothing left He could do to convince me otherwise. As soon as I told God, "There's obviously no point," I got *multiple* text messages from my friend Natalie, literally my spiritual soul sister. She was the woman who listened so keenly to the Lord and was always on point because she was always leaning into God's leading. She somehow always knew when to reach out to me and exactly how to pray for me. She sent me a devotional based on the Book of Ruth that emphasized God's incomparable blessing He unleashes when we love and serve with obedience.

Does God have a sense of humor or what? I was so angry at first because deep down I was hoping He'd finally give me the green light to give up. But of course, He continued to tell me to remain faithful and obedient because at some point there would be this blessing.

Moments later, I mustered up the courage to wipe the tear-stained mascara off my face and walk back downstairs. As soon as I sat down, my family friend Ava came and stood before me. She looked at me, fully unaware of anything I was dealing with, and said, "You know, I'm proud of you. You've always been so devoted to discipline. If anyone can do anything, I know it's you. You've always been so strong."

I was mind-blown. Ava had absolutely no idea of my battle, yet the Lord placed just the words I needed to hear on her heart to share with me. There was absolutely no doubt in my mind that God faithfully provides.

That evening, Allison, one of my mentors, texted me and shared that she had been praying heavily for me during the day. Since high school, she had faithfully pushed me to grow into a strong woman and had never once left my side. Now, she blessed me as she introduced me to Tammy, who then became one of my most cherished mentors and prayer warriors. Tammy shared with me that she had been actively praying the entire Psalm 91 over me, even before we met. As soon as she texted me that, I opened up my daily devotional, and the prayer it told me to pray over myself for May 12 was from *Psalm 91*.

I share this day with you to remind you to never underestimate the power of God, the lengths He will go, and the people He will graciously use to remind you that He is always with you and for you. When you start fervently praying for one another, you open up the door for the Lord to speak to you about how to intercede, and He may end up revealing to you exactly what that person may need.

TAGS

Have you ever moved? If you haven't, have you ever packed up boxes or simply labeled things before you put them away? We label things so we can come back to them by remembering exactly what is in them.

I spent some time thinking about the qualities that make up the purpose and importance of community. I thought that an easy way to remember them is by using the acronym TAGS. When you have the gift of a true solid community, you can eagerly anticipate unpacking these qualities:

Truth
Authenticity
Grace
Servanthood

Truth

True biblical community will not tell you what you want to hear but what the gospel wants you to hear. Sometimes, that truth is not easy to hear at all. If you want to refrain from living in complacency, you need to embrace this form of accountability so your walk will ultimately have credibility. The gospel wasn't given to us to pick and choose from. It was gifted to us to instruct us so we can find direction, which leads to freedom. Solid community will hold you to that standard because they know that encouraging you to become more like Christ and grow your walk with the Lord will never be a waste.

My army of community was never just Team Rhianna or Team Spouse. My army was therefore Team Gospel and Team Marriage. If I were out of line, victimizing myself, or needed to humble myself, they would be bold to tell me, lovingly. I could trust that if they agreed with me, it wasn't just because they were siding with me but because it lined up biblically. That gave me so much peace and left no room for doubt; if I was in the wrong or had room for improvement, they would carry me and be that trustworthy accountability. Seek and pursue people whose ultimate mission is to help mold you to become more like Christ.

Instead, we will speak the truth in love, growing in every way more and more like Christ, who is the head of his body, the church.

—Eph. 4:15

If you listen to constructive criticism,
you will be at home among the wise.

—Prov. 15:31

Authenticity

Authenticity means being able to be completely yourself—intentional and real. A lot of us fear being real and transparent because there's the potential that we may be judged. We long to be loved but worry if people see a certain side of us, a side we ourselves don't even like, we won't be good enough or worthy enough. When you miss out on choosing to live authentically, you miss out on the greatest opportunity to be fully loved and known.

Genuine community is designed to support one another to be able to freely live out the person God created you to be—the good, the bad, and the ugly. People who are part of that community love without condemnation and embrace with acceptance.

For me, I didn't have to live in shame because of my faults, failures, or sin struggles. I was able to freely share the deepest depths of my heart because I knew they'd take what I laid before them and help me fight through those things to look more like Christ, completely judgment-free. My community faithfully accepted me for me and loved me in the same way Christ called them to. As community, we are all called to acknowledge that we're mutually sinners and equally make mistakes because we are all part of a fallen human race.

Grace

Community is your family. Just like family, you're bound to experience conflicts and, at times, butt heads. Overall, the ultimate goal of community is to reconcile and maintain unity.

Again, we all make mistakes. Sometimes we unintentionally hurt one another or allow selfishness to drive a wedge between us. What's so incredibly important to remember is that Christ died for reconciliation. None of us are worthy to be died for, but because Christ saw us as the prize of His eyes, He knew we couldn't fully experience grace and forgiveness without the ministry of reconciliation.

All this is from God, who reconciled us to himself through Christ and gave us the ministry of reconciliation.

—2 Cor. 5:18 NIV

Just as we're called to forgive and love one another, we're also called as brothers and sisters in Christ to hold one another accountable to reconcile with one another. Reconciling is putting past hurts aside, owning your own faults, giving one another the same grace freely gifted to you, and beholding a willing heart that chooses to say, "I want to love you and make this right with you."

Reconciling may not always be easy, and sometimes it isn't possible if one party is completely unwilling. As a follower of Jesus Christ, you need to fight to do all you can to reconcile because it's biblically what you're called to do. The rest of your community should also be there to support you.

"If your brother or sister sins, go and point out their fault, just between the two of you. If they listen to you, you have won them over. But if they will not listen, take one or two others along, so that 'every matter may be established by the testimony of two or three witnesses.' If they still refuse to listen, tell it to the church; and if they refuse to listen even to the church, treat them as you would a pagan or a tax collector."

—Matt. 18:15–17 NIV

Come before one another with a repentant heart, and remember that your mission in community is to grow in unity by becoming more like Christ. Choose to give one another grace because it was powerfully and undeservingly given to you.

Servanthood

One of the greatest blessings community brings is the ability to serve one another. You have the opportunity to fellowship with one another in all aspects of life through the praises and the storms. In our darkest, scariest moments, there is something so powerful in knowing that someone is there to carry you when you no longer have the strength to stand.

Sometimes that looks like complete sacrifice by dropping everything just to be there to support your brother or sister in Christ. It may include going out of your way just to be a hug or a listening ear. It may also be simply telling someone, "I'm here."

No matter how large or small the sacrifice may be in serving one another, being able to do it is genuinely a gift. You bless one another by being Jesus to one another. Serving is an act of love and worship for the Lord. You can freely bless and give unto others because of everything He freely gave to you. Nothing can compare to the powerful love you continue to bind together as you lay yourselves down and serve one another.

"For even the Son of Man came not to be served but to serve others and to give his life as a ransom for many."

—Mark 10:45

Worth More Than Gold

On the evening of **September 6, 2018**, I was sitting on my balcony spending quiet time with the Lord. I kept messing with the ring on my finger and saw there was a very small number engraved on the inside of my band. It ended up being the number of karats in my ring. Out of curiosity, I searched online for the science behind karats (nerd, I know).

Gold in its absolute purest form is 24 karats. What is so interesting is that in its purest form, gold has to be mixed with other metals to strengthen it because it is far too soft on its own.[1]

That made me reflect on how it directly relates to what community does for you. Even when you feel like your walk with the Lord is on fire, you still will not be nearly as strong without community alongside you. My biblical community physically, spiritually, and emotionally carried me when I was incredibly weak. They loved me like Christ in the most incredible forms of sacrificial love.

They served me by:

- Bringing me meals
- Taking me to dinner
- Driving me to church
- Filling me up with scripture
- Praying over me and with me at any and all times and hours of the day
- Talking with me for relentless hours of phone calls and conversations filled with patience and grace, demanding that I never doubt the goodness and faithfulness of God
- Bri wrapping her arms around me and holding my hand during my first time in church alone so I physically wouldn't collapse in complete sorrow
- John and Natalie graciously dropping everything and driving me to the emergency room after my terrifying car accident; Scott and Emily selflessly driving me to my follow-up doctor appointments
- Zach and Bri generously giving me and my crazy dogs a home to live in

1. "What Is a Carat, and How Does It Relate to a Karat?" How-StuffWorks, https://science.howstuffworks.com/dictionary/geology-terms /question64.htm.

And this is just to name a few. They pushed me to love with agape love. Pushed me to forgive like Christ forgives. Pushed me to fight for life and honor Christ above all things. My friends have inherited jewels in their crowns far more than they can imagine. They gave me a ministry, one I couldn't have had without them.

They are the definition of strength in numbers.

My prayer for you, too, my friends, is that you clothe yourselves in community. Don't be afraid to go out of your comfort zone to reach out, utilize resources, and find people who are willing to support you.

It's important to remain humble and recognize that it's okay not to have it all together on your own. Be authentic, be transparent, be vulnerable, and be willing to be held accountable. God never intended for us to walk through life, especially during our battles, alone.

I know for a fact I could not have made it through my journey if it weren't for community. Those people played such a crucial role. Each of them held a piece of my cross, which made it possible for me to carry the rest of it. I couldn't stand tall as this woman of God without those pieces that each and every one of them carried.

There's a strength that lies in numbers, and those numbers keep you firm. That, my friends, is worth more than gold.

Carry each other's burdens, and in this way you will fulfill the law of Christ.

—Gal. 6:2 NIV

Chapter 7

The Priesthood

I didn't want a life rooted in complacency anymore. Why would I deliberately desire to choose a life that's outlined and held captive within bounds? I now wanted a life that ignited a fire so passionate and bright that I couldn't help but find myself racing to the heavenly throne.

I started envisioning myself racing to the throne and into the arms of my mighty King. The most beautiful embrace of eternity. Jesus robed in white. His arms graciously open wide. Finding myself bowing down before Him and my crown being triumphantly laced upon my head. The crown that gleams and glistens because it is filled with jewels individually symbolizing every time I chose to say, "Yes, Jesus, I'm choosing to follow and obey You."

God blesses those who patiently endure testing and temptation. Afterward they will receive the crown of life that God has promised to those who love him.

—James 1:12

I wanted to live my life in such a way that I could radically, fiercely, and proudly give it right back to Him. I longed to hear my Savior say the words, "Well done, my faithful servant," with the most magnificent beaming smile that could never compare to any other. I wanted a life that empowers. A life that speaks life and beauty into every soul I encounter. A life that mirrors the gospel. A life that declares to Jesus, "I can't wait to become more and more like You and bring all the glory to You."

> You, my friends, are part of the royal priesthood. The royal priesthood is a high calling that shouldn't be considered lightly or taken for granted. I challenge you to develop an understanding of your worth and the calling intricately designed by our mighty God. And I pray that you become empowered to boldly live it out, rid of any doubt that you serve a purpose.

Run Your Race

You don't ever run a race anticipating that you will quit. You run a race with the intent to cross the finish line. The goal and driving force are ultimately to obtain the prize of victory. You have put countless hours of conditioning, training, sacrifice, and intense discipline into preparing for the race, which has equipped you with strength, endurance, and perseverance.

What about the opposite? If you never trained for your race and showed up at the starting line, you wouldn't understand how to pace yourself. Once the gunshot was fired, you would immediately take off, flooded with adrenaline pumping through your veins and ready to give it all you have. You would try to stay in first place, but as time passed, you would start to notice that the runners who are steady and slightly behind start to pass you.

What happens when your strength starts to fade and you left all your driving or motivating factors at the starting line?

Anxiety starts to kick in. There's not much more you can give. More and more people start to pass you, and you're completely unsure what to do. You're tired. Your muscles are starting to give out. Exhaustion is finally setting in. You start to waver, and more than likely, you won't finish your race—at least not in first place.

This is why it's imperative that you learn how to fight to endure and persevere.

According to the *Merriam-Webster Dictionary*, the definition of *endurance* is "the ability to **withstand** hardship or adversity, especially the ability to **sustain** a prolonged stressful effort or activity" (emphasis added).

The dictionary defines *perseverance* as "**continued effort** to do or achieve something **despite** difficulties, failure, or opposition; the action or condition or an instance of persevering: steadfastness" (emphasis added).

Endurance and perseverance go hand in hand. Biblically, we're called to embrace both. Endurance is the discipline you utilize to stretch you outside of your comfort zone. It helps hold you accountable against wavering from your mission because you've been conditioned to keep going. Perseverance is what drives you to maintain motivation to finish your race strong and pulls you through that finish line by reminding you why you started in the first place. Both of them combined is the act of fixing your eyes on the prize.

The race in our lives is the mission God has called us to. We each have our own races, some shorter than others and some much more difficult than others. No matter the race, as God's chosen people, we all have exactly the same prize. Our prize is to glorify Christ in whatever the trial or mission laid out before us.

Therefore, since we are surrounded by a huge crowd of witnesses to the life of faith, let us strip off every weight that slows us down, especially the sin that so easily trips us up. And let us run with endurance the race God has set before us. We do this by keeping our eye on Jesus, the champion who initiates and perfects our faith.

—Heb. 12:1–2

When you keep your eyes on Christ, anything trying to distract or defeat you cannot possibly compete against the mighty work He will do to intercede for you. He witnesses faithfulness and obedience and longs to bless you for it. He knows you may get tired and burned out, but because He knows your focus is consistently on Him, He will send you encouragement and ignite the deepest desire in you to fight. He also graciously places people on the sidelines to cheer you on and teammates who run alongside you to push you to keep on.

Here's the coolest thing about your team: before setting up a game plan or even starting the race, you are already determined to win because you've got Jesus as your team captain. With Jesus, His name doesn't just give us victory; He *is* our victory. You've got your army of angels fighting and rooting for you and your biblical community to spur you on and run alongside you.

God is the only one who knows what the return will be for your faithful obedience to press on in your race. If you don't see the outcome yet, continue to endure and persevere because He's not finished with you yet. While that may at times seem daunting, the Lord will fulfill His promise and bring everything to perfect completion.

And I am certain that God, who began the good work within you, will continue his work until it is finally finished on the day when Christ Jesus returns.

—Phil. 1:6

Once you cross your finish line, rest assured that He will reveal everything you fought for in His perfect time. Don't look to the left or to the right. Keep your eyes fixed forward on that finish line. You will cross the line into promised eternity, and your crown of jewels will be waiting to be placed on your head. So don't give up, my friend.

I have not achieved it, but I focus on this one thing: Forgetting the past and looking forward to what lies ahead, I press on to reach the end of the race and receive the heavenly prize for which God, through Christ Jesus, is calling us.

—Phil. 3:13–14

Call to Intercede

Have you ever stopped to wonder that maybe God has allowed you to stand in the place you're in to intercede on behalf of someone else? Maybe what you went through really wasn't about what hurt you as much as it was meant to spur something on inside of you. Maybe you crossed paths with that person who wounded you because God had a divine purpose for you to pray for them. What if you were the only person who ever has or diligently will pray for them?

If you were being called to it, would you do it?

June 1, 2018 – Sobbing, I prayed, "God I can't do this anymore. Please let me go." What He did in that moment was drive an even deeper fight in me because He finally revealed to me my deeper calling in the purpose of my mission. As my husband's wife, I had the God-ordained duty to pray for my husband and faithfully stand firm against the working of the enemy. I was to serve as an intercessor on his behalf. From that day forward, I was determined to finish my race and fight for my husband with full force, on my knees, equipped with one of my powerful weapons: prayer.

Let me take you to **August 1, 2018**. Remember how I shared with you about the many times I wanted to give up? Remember those moments that God showed up in radical ways along my journey to convince me to keep fighting? This day was 24 weeks to the day after I was abandoned, and it absolutely blew my mind.

August 1 was special because it was the dating anniversary my husband and I had. Our story from the very beginning was very unique, and if you know it, without a doubt it was God-ordained. On that day, we had our very first date at a coffee shop. I share this detail with you because it ended up playing a role in my story.

Because this was such a special day, I felt led to gather up all my prayer warriors to unite and pray for my husband at the exact same time: **7:24 a.m. and 7:24 p.m.** More than 60 people were praying for my husband's heart at the same time. Throughout my journey, I had witnessed the insane power of prayer, but this day, I could *physically* feel it.

"For where two or three gather in my name, there am I with them."

—Matt. 18:20 NIV

I devoted that entire day to fasting and covering my husband in prayer. Stormie Omartian's book *The Power of a Praying Wife* acted as a secondary lifeline to me because it had powerful prayers for every aspect of my husband's life. On this particular day, I was led and determined to pray the *entire* book over him. I slept only three hours because I knew I was going to have to put in some heavy work to get that book prayed all in one day.

Come 7:00 p.m., I was completely exhausted. I remember walking out of Watermark's Marriage Ministry that night feeling like there was no way I was going to get this thing conquered. As I was leaving and starting to head home, 7:24 p.m. arrived, and my phone blew up with notifications from everyone who was praying with me. I just knew God was moving. I just didn't know how.

Moments later, I had this incredibly random sense of leading that I needed to go to the coffee shop where my husband and I had met and continue praying for him. Initially, I thought this was insane because it was literally so far out of my way, and, like I shared, I was extremely exhausted. Unfortunately, now that I was six months into my journey, I learned not to question God when He tells you to go. So I went.

I finally got to the coffee shop and continued to pray out of my book. Not long after, the staff started closing the shop. Honestly, I was so frustrated because I had no idea why I felt like God had me drive all the way over there to sit for barely 45 minutes to pray. I packed up to leave, beyond ready to get home at that point. As I pulled up to a stoplight, I again had this even stronger sense that I needed to go pray over my husband in the hospital parking lot where he worked. At first, I was in complete denial, and then I thought I was just completely delirious. But again, God said go. So I went.

I turned right at the light to head in the direction of the hospital, and directly to my left was a salon with the exact same name as my husband. Odd, I thought. Continuing down the road, I ended up getting lost (no surprise) and then saw two street signs that were the same as our last name. Then a sermon came on the radio about the prodigal son. I had thought about that story a lot on my journey because it was as though I had a prodigal spouse.

What was going on?

At that point, I was a bit shaken up and honestly terrified to start praying again. I arrived at the hospital, and the parking lot was extremely packed, so I pulled over on the side of the street. I opened *The Power of a Praying Wife*, and the prayers that were next in line, back-to-back, were for "His Repentance" and "His Deliverance"—the two prayers I had prayed diligently over him *every single day*.

The entire 20 minutes I sat there praying, not a single person walked into or out of the hospital. So I closed the book, completely confused as to why in the world I just *had* to be there to pray, and turned the radio back on. I'm not going to lie, I kind of felt like a fool. As I started driving toward the intersection, I looked to my left to check for any cars coming, and—I kid you not—I immediately saw my husband walk a patient out to the car. In that *exact* moment, the song "It's Not Over Yet" by for King & Country began playing.

If my jaw had the capability of hitting the floor when that happened, it would have. What in the world were the odds of that happening? That was the first time I had seen my husband since we were in court in **May**.

I've learned that with the Lord there are no coincidences.

From what I knew about my husband's job, when it was that packed and busy, there was a slim-to-none chance he would have had the time to walk a patient out to the car.

1. The *timing*
   a. I got lost.
   b. I drove 40+ miles.
   c. I went, sat, and prayed at the coffee shop.
2. The *prayers*
3. The *song*

To this day, I'm still not 100 percent sure why God allowed those things to take place that day. Someday, when I get to the other side of eternity, I cannot wait to find out. What I can tell you is what God taught me that day; I had no idea the impact prayers were having and the power of things happening on His time. Only God knows. God ordained all those events to happen at just the right moment to remind me that He can perform *any* miracle, but it has to be in *His* time. The entire situation was out of my control, but I obeyed and prayed.

Many times I complained to my counselor, Wendy, "I feel like my prayers aren't doing anything. I know God is calling me to pray, but I never see anything from it." The most powerful thing she said to me that day was, "Rhianna, but think about where he could be if you weren't the one fervently praying over him every single day. God knew you would be the one to do it, and you did, and you sure won't be the one to quit."

I tell you this story because I'm sure a lot of you have been praying for a person or maybe even several people but still to this day don't see any prayers answered. You cannot quit unless God specifically calls you to do so and you have a peace in your heart. For me, I was released from praying for my husband on **September 30, 2018**, because the very next day I had to sign my covenant away. I no longer would have that same role to play as his wife. God gave me that peace to release him because I had kept up my fight until the very end.

You have no idea what God is using and what seeds you are planting in your person or any people you are diligently praying for. The Holy Spirit is the only one who can water those seeds and grow them in His ordained time.

For God is not unjust. He will not forget how hard you have worked for him and how you have shown your love to him by caring for other believers, as you still do.

—Heb. 6:10

What you can trust is that He hears the prayers of the righteous, and you just may be the person He has chosen to intercede on their behalf. God is capable of changing hearts. You have absolutely no control over another person. What you have control over is the decision you make about how much you will fight to pray for them. You may just be praying for them in moments they desperately need it the most. Someday, they may come to know the Lord in ways they may not have if it weren't for you. Only God knows, but you must stay faithful, pray, and boldly go when God says go.

None of your prayers will ever be a waste, especially your prayers for someone to either come to find the Lord for the first time or come back to Him again from once walking away. **Believe and be honored when and if you are being called to intercede.**

Pray in the Spirit at all times and on every occasion. Stay alert and be persistent in your prayers for all believers everywhere.

—Eph. 6:18

You Are Chosen

I once read a book called *Operating in the Courts of Heaven* by Robert Henderson. The premise of the book was about our divine role as God's chosen royal priesthood and the power we have been given in prayer to intercede. Because all of this was so new to me, my counselor suggested I read it so I could develop a deeper understanding of those areas. This particular quote from the book really empowered me:

> When God responds to His Chosen people, even unredeemed people and societies will be affected, reformed and transformed.... It all begins out of the love of the Bridegroom for His Bride. He will do for the Bride what would not otherwise be done.[1]

Each of us has been given a set purpose, simply because of God's love for us. Before you were even born, the Lord knew the world needed a unique handcrafted person like you or He wouldn't have made you. He created you because He knew you had the ability to leave a mark on this world to be another form of living proof that there is a God who loves each and every person. All our purposes are more than likely different, but none of them are any less significant. What we all do share in common is our God-ordained identity that can never be taken from us.

On **June 24, 2018**, I was battling *hard* against the lies Satan was trying to tell me about my identity. Instead of allowing myself to succumb to them, I went straight to scripture and wrote what God says and who He declares that I am. I kept this on a piece of paper in my Bible and pulled it out every time I started to feel the lies creeping in.

---

1. Robert Henderson, *Operating in the Courts of Heaven* (Robert Henderson Ministries, 2014), 182.

If you have any doubts that your identity is based on being worthy, chosen, free, and redeemed, go straight to these truths and read the scripture references I have listed below:

- The old you has been wiped away (Col. 2:11).
- The old you has been crucified with Christ; therefore, your sin has absolutely no power over you (Rom. 6:1–6).
- You are forgiven (1 John 1:9).
- You are deemed free from any lies and condemnation (Rom. 8:1).
- Christ never has and never will be ashamed of you (Heb. 2:11).
- You have been given the gift of grace (Eph. 2:5).
- You are called to be holy and without blame because of Christ's sacrifice for you (Eph. 1:4).
- All debts against you have been 100 percent cancelled (Col. 1:14).
- Satan has no claim on you (Col. 1:13).
- You were deliberately chosen and placed into Christ because of God's divine hand (1 Cor. 1:30).
- You were intentionally and selflessly bought with an eternal price (1 Cor. 6:19–20).
- You are covered by every spiritual blessing (Eph. 1:3).
- You have a direct line to God because of Jesus (Eph. 2:18).
- You are bold, free, and confident (Eph. 3:12).
- By Christ alone you are deemed worthy and complete (Col. 2:10).

You are a chosen people. You are royal priests, a holy nation, God's very own possession. As a result, you can show others the goodness of God, for he called you out of the darkness into his wonderful light.

—1 Pet. 2:9

Now that you know your identity in Christ, it's also important to know the spiritual gifts you've been blessed with. Each of us has been given very specific gifts, and they may even change over time.

Maybe you've never actually thought about it before. I want to encourage you to read **1 Corinthians 12:1–31** right now. This chapter in the Bible talks about the meaning and purpose of spiritual gifts. If you've never known what your gifts may be, spend time in prayer and ask God to reveal them to you. It may take some time to come to you, or it may immediately be revealed to you. Take a look at your talents, your passions, and the ways you love people best. These were intentionally designed for you and serve a powerful purpose in all you will continue to do.

My prayer is that you can confidently walk away knowing you serve a mighty purpose in this world. I am hopeful that this will empower you to yearn to use the blessings God has given you so you can bless those around you.

God has given each of you a gift from his great variety of spiritual gifts. Use them well to serve one another.

—1 Pet. 4:10

Chapter 8

Walk

On **April 27, 2018**, I had a vivid dream. I was holding a camera in my hands. As time passed, one of my prayers was answered right before me. When I saw it, I quickly grabbed my camera and tried to focus on my answered prayer so I could capture proof that it actually came true. Every time I looked back at the picture, it had disappeared. I took several pictures but couldn't get a single one to actually show what had happened before me. My dream-self was incredibly frustrated. I clearly remember telling God, "Why won't you show me?"

When I woke up, I realized exactly what God was trying to tell me. I knew that my prayer had been answered. So why was I trying to keep getting proof? I believed God was simply telling me I don't have to physically see it to know it's there, that it happened, or that it's going to happen. In the same way, we don't have to fight to see God because He has always been there and always will be. Walk by faith.

For we live by believing and not by seeing.

—2 Cor. 5:7

It was **September 12, 2018**, and I was planning to travel to Savannah, Georgia, for a work conference. That happened to be the week Hurricane Florence was supposed to hit the Atlantic Coast. I remember sitting in the airport waiting to board my flight. All of a sudden, my phone alerted a notification that the governor of Georgia had announced a state of emergency and was encouraging people to evacuate for safety. My heart started racing, and I called the company who was hosting the convention. I was desperately hoping they, too, were planning to evacuate so I would have a legitimate reason to cancel the trip and avoid the weather.

Needless to say, it was not cancelled, and I was still going to Savannah. I was frustrated with the situation because I felt I was endangering my life just for a work conference and could potentially get stuck there if return flights were cancelled. For me, this was a real test of walking in faith because storms literally terrify me. I begrudgingly boarded my flight and prayed, "All right, God, there must be something you have to tell me in Georgia. You probably already know." He is such a good God, and He definitely did know.

To get to the hotel where the convention would take place, I had to take a ferry. That made me feel even safer about the situation, right? Thankfully, the storm was mild, and there were only minimal effects. I departed on my last ferry ride of the trip and just sat in silence. My hair was blowing out of control due to the fierce winds, and I found myself intently staring at the dark, heavy, black clouds and the choppy waves. I was waiting anxiously for what God was going to tell me.

I was captivated by the waves. The storm was ready to break through at any moment, and that's when God finally reached down and grasped hold of my heart. All of a sudden,

I had a profound realization about this old, rustic ferry I was on.

In our storms of life, the Lord serves as our boat captain on our journey. It doesn't matter which gate or opening we choose to walk through to get on the boat; we still get on. It also doesn't matter where we choose to sit. Those things don't matter because ultimately the small, self-made decisions don't change the port where our captain chooses to take us. The captain chooses the exact destination and is the only one with full awareness of the time it takes to arrive there.

This is true even in our times of rebellion when we choose in our own power and free will to jump off the boat. Despite our waywardness, our Captain still throws out the life raft to rescue us. The truth is, no matter how far we choose to jump out or swim off, the Captain never leaves us behind. We come to the end of ourselves as we're stranded in the middle of the water, choosing to either drown or grasp hold of the offer of rescue graciously thrown out to us.

The waters may be incredibly choppy, but our Captain keeps the sail smooth. He keeps it smooth because He alone has the power to conquer all disasters and distractions to safely take us where He has called us. All our Captain calls us to do is sit back peacefully, watch, and wait. He longs for us to admire the beauty that can always be found on the journey. So, then, we should choose to let our Captain steer our ship and trust His promise that He will take us to the destination He deems fit.

Let God move, direct, and lead you. In faith, believe that He has a mighty plan and purpose in exactly where he is taking you.

*And it is impossible to please God without faith. Anyone who
wants to come to him must believe that God exists and that he
rewards those who sincerely seek him.*

—Heb. 11:6

If you would like to read more scriptures about what faith can
do, I encourage you to read all of Hebrews 11. It talks about
the radical leaps of faith God's most faithful people took.
Their blessings wouldn't have come to fruition the way they
did if they hadn't first taken that leap of faith.

He Goes before You

Have you ever used or seen a retractable leash on a dog? They
can either be a saving grace or your worst nightmare. With
my dogs, I tend to prefer retractable leashes because the dogs
usually get more tired when they have the extra freedom to
run. But oh, the nightmare of trying to reel your dogs back
in when they're spiraling out of control or spot the prize of
a sacred squirrel.

The beauty about the leash is that when they do get carried away, I have the ability to reel them back in and get them
under control. It may at times be difficult, depending on why
I'm reeling them in, but I do it because I love them and know
that obedience, discipline, and self-control are best for them.

One day I was walking my dogs along a trail, and they
started to take off running. I couldn't see past the trees or
around the wide corner, and all I knew was that my dogs saw
something I couldn't see.

Then it hit me.

Until we turn the corner or look through the trees to see
what's in front of us, we blindly trust and walk in faith. The
number of times I proclaimed to know what was best for me

can't even compare to the immense number of times God has reminded me that He's already gone ahead of me. We don't know what destination certain paths may lead to, but He does. That is why we can securely rest and trust in what God deems best for us.

As He sees us choosing the path leading to destination sin, He retracts us. As He sees us choosing the path to destination selfishness, He retracts us. As He sees us choose the path to a destination of the world, in His abounding grace and mercy, He retracts us. God loves us so much that when He sees us getting out of control, He fights to pull us back in close. He pulls us back to remind us that we can't do this thing called life without His direction, guidance, and ultimate control. Even when we start to pull in our own direction, God has the incomparable power to retract us and lead us down the trail he's paved just for us.

"We will stay on the main road; we will not turn aside to the right or to the left."

—Deut. 2:27 NIV

I'd be lying if I told you I wasn't scared the moment my dogs took off. Even though I literally couldn't see what potentially lay ahead of me, I ironically had an odd sense of peace at the same time because of who was before me. I trust that my dogs love me, and they would fight for me if there were something dangerous coming that I couldn't see.

So why don't we freely trust God in the same way?
Rest in the truth that God has gone ahead of you and that the battle has been won for you. Choose to peacefully walk and trust in the God who never fails His promises. When you're

walking, you're moving. You're not stuck, and He sure isn't finished with you yet.

Jotham grew powerful because he walked steadfastly before the LORD *his God.*

—2 Chron. 27:6 NIV

Your Mission Doesn't Stop

For me, there was legally an end to my fight. On **October 1, 2018,** I had no choice but to sign away my covenant in divorce. Let me tell you, that day took a lot of prayer to prep me so I would be full of courage to step foot into my attorney's office and be able to sign with that black ballpoint pen. Little did I know that God had a powerful encounter planned for me before stepping foot on that journey.

On the way to my lawyer's office, I stopped by a gas station at the intersection of Maple and Oak Lawn in Dallas. As I got out of my car, an older, frail man approached me. He asked if I had anything to give, and because I always forget to carry cash, I invited him inside so I could buy him a meal. I also thought I could withdraw some cash for him at the ATM. Leave it to me, I forgot my PIN and couldn't get the cash for him.

As I was messing around with the machine, the man walked out of the store. I ran out to find him and apologize because I couldn't help him any further. He thanked me for the food, and I started to walk away. In that moment, I had this overwhelming leading to go back and pray over him.

I approached him again and asked if I could pray for him. When I placed my hand on him, I was filled with an incredible amount of emotion and genuine hurt as I witnessed him struggling. Eventually, I finished choking through my tear-filled prayer and looked up at him. With his soft, crystal-blue eyes, his warm, rugged face lit up, and he said the most beautiful thank you. We parted ways, and a man walking past me who had apparently witnessed this, said, "Thank you. We need more people like you." I tell you, nothing could wipe the massive smile off my face.

It was in that moment that I realized I was no longer concerned that today was the day I was signing away my marriage. God powerfully took hold of my heart. He moved me so significantly with this encounter to remind me that my calling in life is not defined or altered by my circumstances. I get to be the one who defines my circumstances by how I choose to faithfully seek the Lord, serve His people, and do His mission. My ministry doesn't stop because of the trial the enemy used to try to take me down. Instead, it now gets to begin as my brand-new triumph on my next journey. The good news is that God wants do this for you, too!

Where do you feel God is calling you right now?
Nothing you encounter will stop the fight, the mission, and the plan God has for you. I empower you to fight on, my friend.

Show Me Your Scars
We all have scars. Some are more prominent than others, but none of them have a lack of significance.

Our scars tell a story.

Where we've been.
The trauma we've lived.
The fire we've walked through.
The pain once rooted deep within.

Scars usually aren't pretty. We're quick to cover up our scars out of shame or to protect ourselves from the potential of dimming the beauty found within. We don't want people to see them because we don't *only* want to be seen by them.

Our initial response is more than likely to not be proud of them. You may desperately long for people to know there's far more to you than your scars could ever show. Depending on where you've been, you may feel that it's best to never talk about your scars again.

Some scars take form spiritually, emotionally, or, unfortunately, even physically. They may have been inflicted intentionally or subconsciously by your cherished loved ones, your enemies, or even your own self.

We don't have to be proud of where we've been. More times than not, we probably wish those circumstances or decisions that created those scars would have never existed. Our initial responses tend to look like wishing you could just void all of them. It's difficult to look back at the things that significantly wounded you and convince yourself that something good will come out of them, especially when nothing seems to reveal that truth to you. How do you really fight past the shame and choose to proudly say you're going to use it for Jesus's name?

While you don't have to be proud of the events, things, or places that created those scars, I do challenge you to be proud of what they've made you and who you are because of them.

Some scars may be superficial, while others are deep gashes that took what seems to have been forever to mend. Today you could still be praying for them to finally mend. You can rest in the promise that Jesus will heal them and use them by redirecting you on a mission to bring other people to know Him. Look at some of the most profound people in the Bible. Jesus used them as a massive testament to His ministry. You should be encouraged that He longs for His people to come out stronger on the other side because of how they survived their stories.

People long to hear stories of healing and transformation. They grasp for hope by looking at people like you and me who've been through the pain, damage, and massive wounds but have radically transformed the meaning behind them, all because of the healing Jesus did. They desperately desire to know that they, too, can overcome their scars. They need to know that remaining in bondage will never have an end. I know this because in the deepest depths of my journey, I faithfully and desperately searched for hope of healing by listening to other people's testimonies.

I want to share a significant portion of John 20 about Jesus and His scars. When Jesus was resurrected, He came back to see his disciples, and they knew for certain it was Him because of His scars.

As he spoke, he showed them the wounds in his hands and his side. They were filled with joy when they saw the Lord! One of the twelve disciples, Thomas (nicknamed the Twin), was not with the others when Jesus came. They told him, "We have seen the Lord!" But he replied, "I won't believe it unless I see the nail wounds in his hands, put my fingers into them, and place my hand into the wound in his side." Eight days later the disciples were together again, and this time Thomas was with them. The doors were locked; but suddenly, as before, Jesus was standing among them.... Then he said to Thomas, "Put your finger here, and look at my hands. Put your hand into the wound in my side. Don't be faithless any longer. Believe!" "My Lord and my God!" Thomas exclaimed.

—John 20:20, 24–28

When I came across this story, I personally was inspired to write about it from a different perspective of the scars we bear in our own lives. Jesus wasn't ashamed by His scars. He knew His people would know it was *Him* by witnessing the scars He showed them! My friends, why don't we do the same? Why don't we instead take a bold stance and tell the world that our scars are just fruitful testaments that God faithfully fulfills His promises?

Jesus's scars from the cross didn't just define Him by where He had been. They weren't left at the crucifixion; His *resurrection* boldly glorified them! The story of the gospel lives and breathes because it didn't stop at the cross. Jesus was meant to do what God ultimately destined Him to do—to *rise, live,* and *breathe* so He could powerfully live on in each and every one of you.

That's why it's so imperative that you take those scars and plead to Jesus, "Have your way in me." By doing this, you allow Him to powerfully move through you and reveal the good that is meant to come from all that initially wounded you.

Your scars don't define you by where you have been. No, they give you the opportunity to share the gospel by faithfully proclaiming what Jesus has done *within*! Your scars may have caused a considerable amount of pain, and they still may. But friends, it cannot even begin to compete with the testament of what Jesus Christ has done in you and the legacy you now leave behind you.

So show me your scars. Pray and ask the Lord to open up or reveal opportunities for you to boldly and proudly share your story. Continue to walk in victory, knowing that it's all for His glory.

> *Lord, your discipline is good,*
> > *for it leads to life and health.*
> *You restore my health*
> > *and allow me to live!*
> *Yes, this anguish was good for me,*
> > *for you have rescued me from death*
> > *and forgiven all my sins.*

—Isa. 38:16–17

The Mountaintop

On **October 16, 2018**, I had a dream that I was climbing up an extremely tall and steep mountain. It was exhausting, but I finally made it to the peak. When I arrived, there was a man waiting for me, and he ended up proposing to me. Before he did, he wanted to reassure me of the love he had for me and the unending commitment that he was going to be devoted to me. Once I said yes to this mystery man, I woke up from the dream.

When this dream came to me, I wasn't really sure what to make of it. In December, I started to transfer my journal notes into my Google Drive, and God revealed to me what the dream ended up meaning.

The long journey God had me on was essentially that massive mountain, and it sure was a slow, steady 229-day climb. At the top, my reward was awaiting me. It wasn't until I conquered my mountain that I finally understood why my fight was worth it in the end. Something was so high up that I couldn't even begin to see it, yet God knew all along what was ready to bless me. The man in the dream was Jesus all along. He reassured me every step of the way that I could do this journey because He loved me, and His undying commitment to me was to work this all out for good.

Jesus never gave up on me. He will never give up on you, either. His proposal to you is that if you fight to finish your race and conquer your mountain, you will have a rewarding and promised eternity to live alongside Him. I found the glory and promise of Jesus at the top of my toughest battle. He found me—and He finds you—worthy enough to be called His eternal bride.

If we don't fight through the battle and choose the path of becoming more like Jesus, we will completely miss out on the strength and endurance that leads us to witness the eternal beauty that awaits us.

> *"For I am doing something in your own day,*
> *something you wouldn't believe*
> *even if someone told you about it."*
>
> —Hab. 1:5

Victory Awaits

February 14, 2019 marked one year from my being abandoned. That day, my friend Hannah had been so gracious to get us tickets to go see Bethel Music in concert for their Victory Tour. What a sweet gift it was to celebrate Valentine's Day singing praises to my heavenly Father on the very day He rescued me just a year before. There was power ordained in that very day. Just the fact that the tour was called Victory assured me that God was nothing short of present in this big day for me.

As I was driving to Frisco, Texas, to get to the church where the concert was, I had an eerie sense of familiarity for this particular location. Sure enough, I saw the church on my left, and on my right was the *same donut shop* where my husband and I had had our final date—the one I told you about in the beginning of this book. What were the odds that one year after my abandonment I would be in the same location but singing a new song of victory—literally?

I share that story with you to give you hope that your victory waits for you, too. Right now it may seem like you have no clue where God is taking you. I promise you that in His time, He will surprise you with the details to remind you just how far He has carried you. Have hope in what is yet to come.

Take a moment to envision a small mustard seed of hope, and then plant it. With every thunderstorm in life comes a downpour of rain. Without the rain, your seed would not grow into a beautiful tree. Each and every day is a chance to continue to grow in the Lord and bring Him the ultimate glory. Your walk and faith in the Lord may be but a small seed right now, but in time, it will become a blossoming and fruitful tree. Your roots in the Lord will only continue to grow deeper with nurturing faith and will stand firm through the storms.

What will you choose to stand for?
I don't regret standing for my husband and my marriage. I'd do it again—in a heartbeat. I'd do it again because I can freely walk away in victory knowing I did absolutely *everything* in

my human power to reconcile, to honor the Lord, to honor my husband, and to faithfully fulfill my duty as a wife who stood true to her vows and promises until the **very end**. I was blessed with the utmost greatest opportunity to fiercely love that incredible man, and I knew I had married with every fiber of my being in the most radical Christ-like way. In this I was completely transformed, which became the most powerful gift of all.

My prayer for you is that whatever your circumstance or trial, you will find your freedom by trusting in the Lord and choosing to stand firm in faithfulness. Don't live your life in regret by succumbing to the fear of the what-ifs, because greater is He and all His promises.

Now, friends, as we come to part, let's reflect by standing on these truths:

By the blood of Jesus Christ, you are saved.

You can be renewed. You can be redeemed.

You can and will be free.

You can be free of the chains that may have bound you your entire life.

You can be free of the lies.

You can be free to rejoice that you are a beautiful child of God.

You can be free to share the gospel and the incredible testimony the Lord will bless you with.

You can be free to be a complete kingdom shaker.

You can be free of the shame Satan doesn't want you to get rid of.

You *are* free from the grave.

You *are* free from any doubt that you are loved because Jesus chose *you*!

"And you will know the truth, and the truth will set you free."

—John 8:32

As you embark on your newfound journey and you're not quite sure what you can give or how much you can bring, I empower you to approach the throne with lifted hands declaring, "Lord, I give you my everything." Watch and see the work He'll do in you and the incredible story He's going to bring out of you.

"Yet if you devote your heart to him
and stretch out your hands to him,
if you put away the sin that is in your hand
and allow no evil to dwell in your tent,
then, free of fault, you will lift up your face;
you will stand firm and without fear."

—Job 11:13–15 NIV

You've read the words. You've walked and worked through the pages. You've conquered this journey of seeing the freedom found in abandon and surrender. You've witnessed the power of God's mighty love and the beautiful transformation He delights to instill in your heart.

You've attested that your God has won your battles and chosen to make a fierce warrior out of you. You've rested in seeing the tightly knit bond found in establishing community. You've experienced and meditated on His goodness and graces. You've understood why you've been chosen for a higher calling and why it's imperative to keep running your race.

Overall, my prayer is that you've learned and can firmly believe with all your heart that you and your story are absolutely more than worth it.

Now, my friend, go be **Faithfully Fervent**.

"Well done, my good and faithful servant! You have been faithful."

—Matt. 25:21

In Christ and love,
Rhianna Marie

Scripture References by Chapter

CHAPTER 1: ABANDON

"And while he was still a long way off, his father saw him coming. Filled with love and compassion, he ran to his son, embraced him, and kissed him. His son said to him, 'Father, I have sinned against both heaven and you, and I am no longer worthy of being called your son.' But his father said to his servants, 'Quick! Bring the finest robe in the house and put it on him. Get a ring for his finger and sandals for his feet. And kill the calf we have been fattening. We must celebrate with a feast, for this son of mine was dead and has now returned to life. He was lost, but now he is found.'"

—Luke 15:20–24

The LORD is my rock, my fortress, and my savior;
*   my God is my rock, in whom I find protection.*
He is my shield, the power that saves me,
*   and my place of safety.*

—Ps. 18:2

Upon this rock I will build my church, and all the powers of hell will not conquer it.

—Matt. 16:18

No one can serve two masters. For you will hate one and love the other; you will be devoted to one and despise the other. You cannot serve God and be enslaved to money.

—Matt. 6:24

"Bring all the tithes into the storehouse so there will be enough food in my Temple. If you do," says the LORD of Heaven's Armies, "I will open the windows of heaven for you. I will pour out a blessing so great you won't have enough room to take it in! Try it! Put me to the test!"'

—Mal. 3:10

Wherever your treasure is, there the desires of your heart will also be.

—Matt. 6:21

Throw off your old sinful nature and your former way of life, which is corrupted by lust and deception. Instead, let the Spirit renew your thoughts and attitudes. Put on your new nature, created to be like God—truly righteous and holy.

—Eph. 4:22–24

Let us hold tightly without wavering to the hope we affirm, for God can be trusted to keep his promise.

—Heb. 10:23

Even when there was no reason for hope, Abraham kept hoping— believing that he would become the father of many nations. For God had said to him, "That's how many descendants you will have!" And Abraham's faith did not weaken....Abraham never wavered in believing God's promise. In fact, his faith grew stronger, and in this he brought glory to God.

—Rom. 4:18–20

We can rejoice, too, when we run into problems and trials, for we know that they help us develop endurance. And endurance develops strength of character, and character strengthens our confident hope of salvation. And this hope will not lead to disappointment. For we know how dearly God loves us, because he has given us the Holy Spirit to fill our hearts with his love.

—Rom. 5:3–5

Give your burdens to the LORD,
and he will take care of you.
He will not permit the godly to slip and fall.

—Ps. 55:22

You intended to harm me, but God intended it all for good. He brought me to this position so I could save the lives of many people.

—Gen. 50:20

CHAPTER 2: HUMBLED

When we were controlled by our old nature, sinful desires were at work within us, and the law aroused these evil desires that produced a harvest of sinful deeds, resulting in death. But now we have been released from the law, for we died to it and are no longer captive to its power. Now we can serve God, not in the old way of obeying the letter of the law, but in the new way of living in the Spirit. And I know that nothing good lives in me, that is, in my sinful nature. I want to do what is right, but I can't. I want to do what is good, but I don't. I don't want to do what is wrong, but I do it anyway. But if I do what I don't want to do, I am not really the one doing wrong; it is sin living in me that does it.

—Rom. 7:5–6, 18–20

And what was the result? You are now ashamed of the things you used to do, things that end in eternal doom.

—Rom. 6:21

For Christ also suffered once for sins, the righteous for the unrighteous, to bring you to God. He was put to death in the body but made alive in the Spirit.

—1 Pet. 3:18 NIV

People who conceal their sins will not prosper,
*   but if they confess and turn from them, they will receive mercy.*
Blessed are those who fear to do wrong,
*   but the stubborn are headed for serious trouble.*

—Prov. 28:13–14

"Keep on asking, and you will receive what you ask for. Keep on seeking, and you will find. Keep on knocking, and the door will be opened to you. For everyone who asks, receives. Everyone who seeks, finds. And to everyone who knocks, the door will be opened."

—Matt. 7:7–8

Create in me a clean heart, O God.
Renew a loyal spirit within me.

—Ps. 51:10

And some of the wise will fall victim to persecution. In this way,
they will be refined and cleansed and made pure until the time
of the end, for the appointed time is still to come.

—Dan. 11:35

Then the LORD *God formed the man from the dust of the ground.*
He breathed the breath of life into the man's nostrils, and the
man became a living person.

—Gen. 2:7

To all who mourn in Israel, he will give a crown of beauty
for ashes, a joyous blessing instead of mourning, festive praise
instead of despair. In their righteousness, they will be like great
oaks that the LORD *has planted for his own glory.*

—Isa. 61:3

Let your roots grow down into him, and let your lives be built
on him. Then your faith will grow strong in the truth you were
taught, and you will overflow with thankfulness.

—Col. 2:7

"Yes, I am the vine; you are the branches. Those who remain
in me, and I in them, will produce much fruit. For apart from
me you can do nothing."

—John 15:5

You must all be quick to listen, slow to speak, and slow to get angry. Human anger does not produce the righteousness God desires. So get rid of all the filth and evil in your lives, and humbly accept the word God has planted in your hearts, for it has the power to save your souls. But don't just listen to God's word. You must do what it says. Otherwise, you are only fooling yourselves.

—James 1:19–22

Give thanks to the LORD, for he is good!
  His faithful love endures forever.

—Ps. 107:1

CHAPTER 3: BECOMING LOVE

Live a life filled with love, following the example of Christ. He loved us and offered himself as a sacrifice for us, a pleasing aroma to God.

—Eph. 5:2

"You have heard the law that says the punishment must match the injury: 'An eye for an eye, and a tooth for a tooth.' But I say, do not resist an evil person! If someone slaps you on the right cheek, offer the other cheek also. If you are sued in court and your shirt is taken from you, give your coat, too."

—Matt. 5:38–40

We bless those who curse us. We are patient with those who abuse us. We appeal gently when evil things are said about us.

—1 Cor. 4:12–13

"But I say, love your enemies! Pray for those who persecute you!"

—Matt. 5:44

"If the world hates you, remember that it hated me first. The world would love you as one of its own if you belonged to it, but you are no longer part of the world. I chose you to come out of the world, so it hates you."

—John 15:18–19

And he said to David, "You are a better man than I am, for you have repaid me good for evil. Yes, you have been amazingly kind to me today, for when the LORD put me in a place where you could have killed me, you didn't do it. Who else would let his enemy get away when he had him in his power? May the LORD reward you well for the kindness you have shown me today."

—1 Sam. 24:17–19

Make allowance for each other's faults, and forgive anyone who offends you. Remember, the LORD forgave you, so you must forgive others. Above all, clothe yourselves with love, which binds us all together in perfect harmony. And let the peace that comes from Christ rule in your hearts. For as members of one body you are called to live in peace.

— Col. 3:13–15

CHAPTER 4: FULL ARMOR

Therefore, put on every piece of God's armor so you will be able to resist the enemy in the time of evil. Then after the battle you will still be standing firm.

—Eph. 6:13

Even though I walk through the valley of the shadow of death,
        I will fear no evil,
for you are with me;
        your rod and your staff,
        they comfort me.

—Ps. 23:4 ESV

The thief's purpose is to steal and kill and destroy. My purpose is to give them a rich and satisfying life.

—John 10:10

Stay alert! Watch out for your great enemy, the devil. He prowls around like a roaring lion, looking for someone to devour. Stand firm against him, and be strong in your faith. Remember that your family of believers all over the world is going through the same kind of suffering you are.

—1 Pet. 5:8–9

Catch all the foxes,
        those little foxes,
before they ruin the vineyard of love,
        for the grapevines are blossoming!

—Song of Sol. 2:15

"I have told you all this so that you may have peace in me. Here on earth you will have many trials and sorrows. But take heart, because I have overcome the world."

—John 16:33

For God has not given us a spirit of fear and timidity, but of power, love, and self-discipline.

—2 Tim. 1:7

All Scripture is inspired by God and is useful to teach us what is true and to make us realize what is wrong in our lives. It corrects us when we are wrong and teaches us to do what is right. God uses it to prepare and equip his people to do every good work.

—2 Tim. 3:16–17

CHAPTER 5: THE TRENCHES

"The human heart is the most deceitful of all things, and desperately wicked. Who really knows how bad it is?"

—Jer. 17:9

"The LORD will fight for you; you need only to be still."

—Exod. 14:14 NIV

"Be still, and know that I am God!"

—Ps. 46:10

*A single day in your courts
    is better than a thousand anywhere else!
I would rather be a gatekeeper in the house of my God
    than live the good life in the homes of the wicked.*

—Ps. 84:10

These trials will show that your faith is genuine. It is being tested as fire tests and purifies gold—though your faith is far more precious than mere gold. So when your faith remains strong through many trials, it will bring you much praise and glory and honor on the day when Jesus Christ is revealed to the whole world.

—1 Pet. 1:7

"Blessed is anyone who does not stumble on account of me."

—Matt. 11:6 NIV

We were crushed and overwhelmed beyond our ability to endure, and we thought we would never live through it. In fact, we expected to die. But as a result, we stopped relying on ourselves and learned to rely only on God, who raises the dead. And he did rescue us from mortal danger, and he will rescue us again. We have placed our confidence in him, and he will continue to rescue us. And you are helping us by praying for us. Then many people will give thanks because God has graciously answered so many prayers for our safety.

—2 Cor. 1:8–11

The Lord took hold of me, and I was carried away by the Spirit of the Lord to a valley filled with bones. He led me all around among the bones that covered the valley floor. They were scattered everywhere across the ground and were completely dried out. Then he said to me, "Speak a prophetic message to these bones and say, 'Dry bones, listen to the word of the Lord! This is what the Sovereign Lord says: Look! I am going to put breath into you and make you live again! I will put flesh and muscles on you and cover you with skin. I will put breath into you, and you will come to life. Then you will know that I am the Lord.'"

—Ezek. 37:1–2, 4–6

When Pharaoh finally let the people go, God did not lead them along the main road that runs through Philistine territory, even though that was the shortest route to the Promised Land. God said, "If the people are faced with a battle, they might change their minds and return to Egypt." So God led them in a roundabout way through the wilderness toward the Red Sea. Thus the Israelites left Egypt like an army ready for battle.

—Exod. 13:17–18

"The fields that used to lie empty and desolate in plain view of everyone will again be farmed. And when I bring you back, people will say, 'This former wasteland is now like the Garden of Eden! The abandoned and ruined cities now have strong walls and are filled with people!' Then the surrounding nations that survive will know that I, the LORD, have rebuilt the ruins and replanted the wasteland."

—Ezek. 36:34–36

But the Lord stands beside me like a great warrior.
  Before him my persecutors will stumble.
  They cannot defeat me.

—Jer. 20:11

CHAPTER 6: STRENGTH IN NUMBERS

As a face is reflected in water,
  so the heart reflects the real person.

—Prov. 27:19

Rejoice with those who rejoice; mourn with those who mourn.

—Rom. 12:15 NIV

If sinners entice you,
    turn your back on them!
...don't go along with them!
    Stay far away from their paths."

—Prov. 1:10, 15

Instead, we will speak the truth in love, growing in every way more and more like Christ, who is the head of his body, the church.

—Eph. 4:15

If you listen to constructive criticism,
    you will be at home among the wise.

—Prov. 15:31

All this is from God, who reconciled us to himself through Christ and gave us the ministry of reconciliation.

—2 Cor. 5:18 NIV

"If your brother or sister sins, go and point out their fault, just between the two of you. If they listen to you, you have won them over. But if they will not listen, take one or two others along, so that 'every matter may be established by the testimony of two or three witnesses.' If they still refuse to listen, tell it to the church; and if they refuse to listen even to the church, treat them as you would a pagan or a tax collector."

—Matt. 18:15–17 NIV

"For even the Son of Man came not to be served but to serve others and to give his life as a ransom for many."

—Mark 10:45

Carry each other's burdens, and in this way you will fulfill the law of Christ.

—Gal. 6:2 NIV

CHAPTER 7: THE PRIESTHOOD

God blesses those who patiently endure testing and temptation. Afterward they will receive the crown of life that God has promised to those who love him.

—James 1:12

Therefore, since we are surrounded by a huge crowd of witnesses to the life of faith, let us strip off every weight that slows us down, especially the sin that so easily trips us up. And let us run with endurance the race God has set before us. We do this by keeping our eye on Jesus, the champion who initiates and perfects our faith.

—Heb. 12:1–2

And I am certain that God, who began the good work within you, will continue his work until it is finally finished on the day when Christ Jesus returns.

—Phil. 1:6

I have not achieved it, but I focus on this one thing: Forgetting the past and looking forward to what lies ahead, I press on to reach the end of the race and receive the heavenly prize for which God, through Christ Jesus, is calling us.

—Phil. 3:13–14

For where two or three gather in my name, there am I with them.

—Matt. 18:20 NIV

For God is not unjust. He will not forget how hard you have worked for him and how you have shown your love to him by caring for other believers, as you still do.

—Heb. 6:10

Pray in the Spirit at all times and on every occasion. Stay alert and be persistent in your prayers for all believers everywhere.

—Eph. 6:18

You are a chosen people. You are royal priests, a holy nation, God's very own possession. As a result, you can show others the goodness of God, for he called you out of the darkness into his wonderful light.

—1 Pet. 2:9

God has given each of you a gift from his great variety of spiritual gifts. Use them well to serve one another.

—1 Pet. 4:10

CHAPTER 8: WALK

For we live by believing and not by seeing.

—2 Cor. 5:7

And it is impossible to please God without faith. Anyone who wants to come to him must believe that God exists and that he rewards those who sincerely seek him.

—Heb. 11:6

"We will stay on the main road; we will not turn aside to the right or to the left."

—Deut. 2:27 NIV

Jotham grew powerful because he walked steadfastly before the LORD his God.

—2 Chron. 27:6 NIV

As he spoke, he showed them the wounds in his hands and his side. They were filled with joy when they saw the Lord! One of the twelve disciples, Thomas (nicknamed the Twin), was not with the others when Jesus came. They told him, "We have seen the Lord!" But he replied, "I won't believe it unless I see the nail wounds in his hands, put my fingers into them, and place my hand into the wound in his side." Eight days later the disciples were together again, and this time Thomas was with them. The doors were locked; but suddenly, as before, Jesus was standing among them. ...Then he said to Thomas, "Put your finger here, and look at my hands. Put your hand into the wound in my side. Don't be faithless any longer. Believe!" "My Lord and my God!" Thomas exclaimed.

—John 20:20, 24–28

Lord, your discipline is good,
for it leads to life and health.
You restore my health
and allow me to live!
Yes, this anguish was good for me,
for you have rescued me from death
and forgiven all my sins.

—Isa. 38:16–17

For I am doing something in your own day,
something you wouldn't believe
even if someone told you about it.

—Hab. 1:5

And you will know the truth, and the truth will set you free.

—John 8:32

"Yet if you devote your heart to him
and stretch out your hands to him,
if you put away the sin that is in your hand
and allow no evil to dwell in your tent,
then, free of fault, you will lift up your face;
you will stand firm and without fear."

—Job 11:13–15 NIV

"Well done, good and faithful servant! You have been faithful."

—Matt. 25:21

References

Carroll, Jackie. "Dry and Brittle Trees—What Causes Tree Branch Breaking and Brittleness." April 4, 2018. Gardening Know How. https://www.gardeningknowhow.com/ornamental/trees/tgen /dry-brittle-tree-branches.htm.

Cutler, Karen Davis. "How to Prune Your Vines and Other Climbing Plants." September 8, 2003. Brooklyn Botanic Garden. https:// www.bbg.org/gardening/article/pruning_plants_that_ascend.

Henderson, Robert. *Operating in the Courts of Heaven.* (Robert Henderson Ministries, 2014).

Rao, Joe. "Rainbows: How They Form & How to See Them." March 15, 2011. LiveScience. www.livescience.com/30235 -rainbows-formation-explainer.html.

"What Is a Carat, and How Does It Relate to a Karat?" HowStuff-Works. https://science.howstuffworks.com/dictionary/geology -terms/question64.htm.

Acknowledgments

I could not be standing tall and firm as the woman of God I am today without the incredible people who faithfully walked and fought alongside me. "Thank you" cannot even come close to the utmost genuine gratitude and appreciation I have for each of you. What you've done for me and continue to do for me today is worthy of so much praise.

Thank you to my incredible counselor, Wendy, for always fighting for me to become the woman of God I was created to be.

Thank you to my parents who were willing to make sacrifices to help support me along my journey.

Watermark Church in Dallas, I thank you for being a church that biblically holds its members accountable to faithfully living out the gospel and for honoring the sacred covenant of marriage. I thank you for providing me a community, leadership in the church, and ministries, especially ReEngage marriage ministry, as resources to grow me as a strong, faithful woman.

Foundation Married Community Group—Zach and Bri, John and Natalie, Scott and Emily, and leaders Spencer and Laura—you have exemplified the genuine love of Christ and relentless pursuit of honoring the Lord as my community group. Thank you for fighting for my marriage, always pushing me to love and look like Christ, and showing Christ-like love and endless prayer to and for my husband.

Thank you to my friends Montoya and Chris R., Allison S., Tammy P., Janae P., Emily G., Ariel B., Susan W., Melissa H., Hope L., Jordan L., Crystal and Garrett, John M., Chase W., Miguel B., Crystal A., Jaimy S., Hannah and Cameron, Hannah and Campbell, the Cott family, and the Powers family.

Thank you to my faithful friends and the brothers and sisters in Christ I gained along the way: Becky and Kelly, Jessica and Seth, Candice and Mitch, and Lauren and Chase.

Thank you to my Watermark Women's Fall 2018 Bible Study group, especially Lauren S. and Kimberly M.

Thank you to my co-workers who made work a safe place and one of encouragement: Shannon G. and Seth, Caitilin N., Jenn C., Kelsey D., Emily Z., Christa T., Christine C., Taylor W., McKyna B., and Dakota W.

Thank you to every person in the community who prayed for me and my marriage by shared prayer requests.

Finally, thank you to everyone who helped support my ministry financially to make God's mission possible.

www.ingramcontent.com/pod-product-compliance
Lightning Source LLC
Chambersburg PA
CBHW051428090426
42737CB00014B/2864